*Early Christian
Spirituality*

# Sources of Early Christian Thought

A series of new English translations of patristic texts essential to an understanding of Christian theology
WILLIAM G. RUSCH, EDITOR

The Christological Controversy
Richard A. Norris, Jr., translator/editor

The Trinitarian Controversy
William G. Rusch, translator/editor

Theological Anthropology
J. Patout Burns, S.J., translator/editor

The Early Church and the State
Agnes Cunningham, SSCM, translator/editor

Biblical Interpretation in the Early Church
Karlfried Froehlich, translator/editor

Early Christian Spirituality
Charles Kannengiesser, editor

Understandings of the Church
E. Glenn Hinson, translator/editor

# *Early Christian Spirituality*

Translated by PAMELA BRIGHT
Edited by CHARLES KANNENGIESSER

FORTRESS PRESS
PHILADELPHIA

**Library of Congress Cataloging-in-Publication Data**

Early Christian spirituality.

  (Sources of early Christian thought)
  Bibliography: p.
    1. Spirituality—History of doctrines—Early church, ca. 30–600–Sources.  2. Christian life—Early church, ca. 30–600–Sources.  I. Bright, Pamela, 1937–  .
II. Kannengiesser, Charles. III.  Series.
BR195.C5E37 1986     248'.09'015     86–45226
ISBN O–8006–1416–X

2542C86   Printed in the United States of America   1–1416

# Contents

# Series Foreword

Christianity has always been attentive to historical fact. Its motivation and focus have been, and continue to be, the span of life of one historical individual, Jesus of Nazareth, seen to be a unique historical act of God's self-communication. The New Testament declares that this Jesus placed himself within the context of the history of the people of Israel and perceived himself as the culmination of the revelation of the God of Israel, ushering into history a new chapter. The first followers of this Jesus and their succeeding generations saw themselves as part of this new history. Far more than a collection of teachings or a timeless philosophy, Christianity has been a movement in, and of, history, acknowledging its historical condition and not attempting to escape it.

Responsible scholarship now recognizes that Christianity has always been a more complex phenomenon than some have realized, with a variety of worship services, theological languages, and structures of organization. Christianity assumed its variegated forms on the anvil of history. There is a real sense in which history is one of the shapers of Christianity. The view that development has occurred within Christianity during its history has virtually universal acceptance. But not all historical events had an equal influence on the development of Christianity. The historical experience of the first several centuries of Christianity shaped subsequent Christianity in an extremely crucial manner. It was in this initial phase that the critical features of the Christian faith were set; a vocabulary was created, options of belief and practice were accepted or rejected. Christianity's understanding of its God and of the person of Christ, its worship life, its communal structure, its understanding of the human condition, all were largely resolved in this early period, known as the time of the church fathers or the patristic church (A.D. 100–700). Because this is the case, both those individuals who bring a faith commitment to Christianity and those interested in it as a major religious and historical phenomenon must have a special regard for what happened to the Christian faith in these pivotal centuries.

The purpose of this series is to allow an English-reading public to gain firsthand insights into these significant times for Christianity by making available in a modern, readable English the fundamental sources which chronicle how Christianity and its theology attained their normative character. Whenever possible, entire patristic writings or sections are presented. The varying points of view within the early church are given their opportunity to be heard. An introduction by the translator and editor of each volume describes the context of the documents for the reader.

Hopefully these several volumes will enable their readers to gain not only a better understanding of the early church but also an appreciation of how Christianity of the twentieth century still reflects the events, thoughts, and social conditions of this earlier history.

It has been pointed out repeatedly that the problem of doctrinal development within the church is basic to ecumenical discussion today. If this view is accepted, along with its corollary that historical study is needed, then an indispensable element of true ecumenical responsibility has to be a more extensive knowledge of patristic literature and thought. It is with that urgent concern, as well as a regard for a knowledge of the history of Christianity, that *Sources of Early Christian Thought* is published.

WILLIAM G. RUSCH

# I.

## Introduction

Christian spirituality reflects the radiance of Christian faith in daily life. It implies theology, and calls for asceticism, but has its own definition. It matures in the consciousness by means proper to itself—that is, through charisms and intuitions of basic and verifiable evidence of the meaning of human life, as well as through convictions about another life, a life transfigured, redeemed from evil and freed from death, a life in God. Thus, any spiritual message delivered by a Christian opens new doors into divine transcendency, in marking the steps, and describing the motives, and in celebrating the never-complete achievements which lead the believers through such doors.

Christian spirituality today may be regulated by well-defined rules of traditional piety, or by assumptions born of newly discovered forms of freedom with regard to these rules. Nevertheless, it would always claim to be identifiable as Christian because it is rooted in the New Testament and nurtured in the primordial traditions of the church.

The present collection of texts covers the main trends of Christian spirituality from the second to the seventh century. There is a distinctive feature common to the nine documents collected: they all belong to a time when the Christian churches in the east and the west of the Roman Empire, even in the later period when barbarian kingdoms had overruled the Roman administration in many areas, kept a sense for their essential unity. "Ecumenical," at that time, was identical with being part of the one church in the whole of the so-called civilized world. Later on, in the Byzantine and in the Latin Middle Ages, Christian spirituality became more strictly confined to local mentalities and molded by monastic rules. In the process of its own development, it assimilated aspects of the popular religion in each place and so soon split up into a bewildering variety of devotions with their own practices and their peculiar esthetics. In modern times, this richly differentiated picture of Christian spirituality, inherited from the medieval cultures, has been somewhat overshadowed by the inner history of the older churches and the new Christian denominations issuing from the Reformation. Now spread over many regions of the planet, it tends to be more and more disconnected from the past of European Christianity. That the next global horizon of Christian spiritualities would be Asian was prophetically perceived by Thomas Merton. Our own times have seen the intense acculturating dynamics in Africa and in South America able to generate a shape already recognizable as that of a non-European-based spirituality. The hopes of individuals and communities, facing the future of the churches in this regard, may be nurtured in a fruitful way if such hopes are confirmed by the appropriate interpretation of Christian spirituality at its very inception, when the inventiveness and plurality of its cultural creativity are witnessed by the authors whose essays are collected in this volume.

A lucid assessment of early sources in the realm of doctrinal and religious traditions through centuries, if not millennia, demands cautious treatment. What will be exemplified in this volume is only a very small part of the spiritual treasure accumulated by the men and women who confessed Christ in the ancient church. First of all, the collected sources are all *literary* by nature, whereas nothing is more fitting to an authentic experience of Christian spirituality than a devoted and contemplative silence. If circumstances impose it, or if silence itself becomes overwhelmed by its inner mystical tension, one would expect at most some kind of *oral* communication: mystical tension, the spontaneous song of the soul or the outcry of a prayer, or the confession of Christian beliefs. On the other hand, it is clear that literature belongs to a less immediate mode of sharing the experiences and attitudes generated by religious fervor. And what should one say of the *silent*, but more eloquent witnesses of Christian devotion engraved with a unique artistry in the cronstones, the famous khatchkars, still planted on the hills and in the valleys of windy highlands in Soviet Armenia? From the fourth century on, at the other end of ancient Christianity, a similar non-figurative response may be seen in consecrated stones, like those called Fahan Mura Slab and Kilfountain or Reask Pillar, in the northern and southern corners of early Christian Ireland. What of the message of all the paintings and frescoes hidden in the Roman catacombs, or of miraculously preserved mosaics from the fourth or fifth century, still glittering in the Mediterranean sunshine on the walls of ancient basilicas? In St. Catherine's monastery at Mount Sinai, a huge set of very old materials was recovered by the local monks on 26 May 1975. As these treasures contain musical notations of a very early period in which such data was lacking previously, new insight may be gained into popular expression of early Christian spirituality.

Our present documentation in this volume not only is restricted to literary forms but is also further limited by a number of deliberate choices. Except for the letter on *The Martyrs of Lyons* (chap. 3), the texts presented were all written by individuals. They transmit their personal experiences, or they let us hear their singular convictions in spiritual matters. For reasons of convenience, no mystical documents produced by institutions or referring directly to institutions were taken into account. These documents would obviously provide enough material for volumes of their own. For the same reason, liturgical texts and monastic rules are excluded, as are synodal statements concerning Christian spirituality. But the individual celebration of spiritual gifts and mystical experience in the early church was never far from the poetic forms of local liturgies, as in the *Odes of Solomon* (chap. 2) and in *Romanos the Melodist* (chap. 9); and in his own very personal style, Ambrose of Milan, in his letter *Concerning Virgins* (chap. 7), introduces us into the nascent fervor of Latin Christian monasticism.

## SELECTIONS FROM ODES OF SOLOMON

The *Odes of Solomon* were discovered in an eastern region of Syria in 1905 by Rendel Harris and first published by him in 1909. Mainly known in a Syriac translation, the forty-two odes were originally written in Greek. They had provided a liturgical hymnbook for a Christian community probably as early as the middle of the second century. Their attribution to Solomon is purely accidental because they were found bound together with the Jewish apocryphal book called *Psalms of Solomon*, which dates from the first century B.C. Despite an intense and ongoing scholarship dedicated to them, the *Odes* have not yet reached the broader audience they deserve. Their mystical poetry has often

3

been suspected, and no doubt with some good reasons, as being of a gnostic flavor. But two observations are decisive on this point.

First, there is nothing in the *Odes* which would contradict the basic consensus of the apostolic churches in the second century; in particular, their mystical message is heavily dependent on psalmic imagery, and their obvious Semitic overtones never imply the slightest rejection of the canonical writings of the Old Testament. Even if typed as gnostic, the *Odes* vindicate their claim for being considered as truly Christian, along with Johannine literature, the Letters of Ignatius of Antioch, and Christian apocryphas of the time. Second, the *Odes* represent an authentic masterpiece of spiritual poetry. Their message celebrates the highest values of human love and of religious self-dedication in focusing on baptismal symbols and on communitarian liturgies of praise for baptismal rebirth. The intrinsic beauty of their language, given its "gnostic" inspiration, speaks immediately to contemporary baptismal experience.

Odes 37 and 40 belong to an "autobiographical" series of Odes with Odes 3, 14, 20, and 26. The odist introduces himself with extended hands in the old Christian attitude of prayer. Honey, milk, and running water are among the best-known baptismal symbols in the ancient churches. The exulting hopes of the faithful are expressed in the lyrical mode of the Song of Songs. Grace is given for the sacramental experience of salvation. The final "Hallelujah" may be considered as the congregation's response to the odist's liturgical song.

A complementary reading to the *Odes of Solomon* would include another series of them, dedicated to a more doctrinal celebration of baptism: Odes 6, 10, 11, 15, and 30. In a remarkable christological series, Christ takes the place of the odist and sings in the first person his own paschal mystery: Odes 8 and 41 are hymns for Easter Sunday, Ode 10 celebrates Christ as sent by the Father, and Ode 31 gives a voice to Jesus exposed to the offenses of his jailer. Odes 17 and 42 are the victorious hymns of the Risen One, whereas Odes 27 and 28 insist on other aspects of salvific realities as celebrated at Easter.

Among the main spiritual themes recurrent in the Odes, the central notion of a fulfilled salvation due to Christ generates a whole range of expressions concerning the "newness of the spirit" (Ode 11), the "new birth" experienced in baptism and in

Christian faith (Odes 15, 17, and 21), the newness of the Odes themselves speaking in the person of the Savior (Ode 31) and his saved congregation (Ode 41).

## THE MARTYRS OF LYON

The letter on *The Martyrs of Lyon* was sent in the second century from Lyon, or Lugdunum, of the so-called Three Gauls (*Tres Galliae*), in other words, three among the provinces of Gaul under Roman administration at that time. It was addressed to Christian communities in the Roman province of Asia, in modern Turkey, soon after a local pogrom had devastated the small Christian minority in A.D. 177. The letter is recorded in the *Ecclesiastical History,* Book V, by Eusebius of Caesarea, the founder of church history in the early fourth century.

Lyon was in the second century a lively and important economic center, with a rich rural hinterland, commercial activities on the Rhone River open to international exchanges, and its own forms of business, mainly textiles, oil, wine, and cereals. Religious groups of all sorts, professional corporations, proliferating small shops, patrons, and worker unions, all blending together, contributed to the prosperity of the city.

Each year the sixty "nations" of the Three Gauls would send delegates to the federal capital, where they held a council from the first day of August on and attended festivities in honor of the emperors. In fact, there were two emperors, Marcus Aurelius and Commodus, in office between A.D. 176 and 177, when the Senate of Rome allowed the higher religious officials of the Three Gauls the expedient of replacing the gladiators in the circus games with convicts sentenced to death. In A.D. 176, the few Christians of Lyon had refused to share religious festivals with the populace in honor of Marcus Aurelius after he had returned from a victorious campaign along the Danube and in the Orient. The federal cult of the divinity symbolizing Rome and of the emperors, divinized either posthumously or living, was a well-established and highly popular institution of public life in the Three Gauls.

So much for the social and political context. Who were the Christian martyrs? Seventeen names of forty-eight, according to their traditional counting, seem to be Greek, which is hardly more of a percentage than what statistics signal for the average population. Their professions? Servants, a physician, an advocate, ministers of the cult. A few among them are easier to identify. Alexander came from Phrygia, in Asia Minor, several years before the persecution. Greek and oriental physicians like him were common in the West. He was well-known in town. Attalus was a Roman citizen whose home was Pergamum in modern Turkey. Being rich, he had patronized the Christian community in Lyon. Blandina was a slave belonging to the indigenous population. She had no specific function in the community, but she assumed leadership of the martyr band. Perhaps she was a sister of Ponticus, fifteen years old when he was killed, and also a slave. Sanctus was a deacon of Vienne, near Lyon. It seems that he was in charge of that local church. Vettius Epagathus was probably a freed slave or the son of such a slave, belonging to the famous Roman family of the Vettii, and he was of Greek origin. As an advocate, he was for a time of great help to the Christians and held in high esteem by them. There is a possibility that he belonged to the local nobility. At any event, he was beheaded in the status of a Roman citizen.

The heightened sense of drama which pervades the whole letter marks its opening sentence: "There can be no adequate description. . . . " The stage is set immediately with Satan as the principal actor, and with the episodes of the persecution as a prelude to the day of judgment. Just as in the Book of Maccabees, angelic warriors are fighting beside God's champions. The martyrs are "athletes" of God, their powerful confession of faith being strikingly contrasted to their physical frailty. They are full of Christ's spirit, "strengthened by the heavenly fountain whose lifegiving waters flow from the side of Christ." Exemplified in a spectacular way by Blandina, each of them, like Pothinus, acted "as if he (or she) were Christ himself." Blandina hung there "in the form of a cross," she "had put on the mighty and invincible warrior, Christ." And like the mother of the martyrs in Maccabees, she incorporated in herself the heroic faith of the whole community, this time the faith of the church, "the Virgin Mother." Her companions were, through martyrdom, "conceived again and quickened in the womb," their violent death giving them a direct access to the resurrection, and to a new life in Christ. This central theme of the letter is admirably summarized in its ending paragraph: "They asked for life, and he gave it to them, and they shared it with their neighbor when they went forth to God in complete triumph."

The letter combines grim realism with intense spiritual lyrics. With the vivid imagery of the cosmic battle against "the Adversary," or "the Beast," reminiscent of Revelation, it enunciates a careful teaching about what true martyrs really mean for the church, namely, "joy, peace, harmony and love." It would be worth complementing the reading of this letter with other documents of the genre it inaugurated in Christian literature, such as *The Martyrdom of Polycarp*, or *The Martyrdom of Perpetua and Felicitas*.

## CLEMENT OF ALEXANDRIA

### *Exhortation to the Greeks*

In the earliest Christian communities, spirituality inspired poems and songs which were welcomed in liturgical assemblies, as witnessed by the *Odes of Solomon*. More dramatically, it inspired heroic behavior in the bloody arenas where women and men were exposed to wild beasts because they confessed Christ. But as soon as educated people entered the church in growing numbers, Christian spirituality assumed a different stance in becoming a learned experience and a celebration of more intellectual values. Apologetics against Jewish opposition or pagan philosophers, such as those of Justin of Rome around A.D. 160, were properly speaking a matter of scholarly skills applied to the needed defense of Christianity. They should not be confounded with spirituality. But still, they might be filled with the vibrancy and the lyrics proper to testimonies in favor of Christian mysticism as was the case in the anonymous *Letter to Diognetus*, written during the second half of the second century in the highly sophisticated urban setting of Alexandria in Egypt.

It was at that time that Clement, already an adult, converted to Christianity in this same city. His quest for religious truth had led him from Athens to southern Italy, and from there to Palestine before he found the kind of evidence he needed in listening to an old Alexandrian teacher Panthenus, himself a convert and a philosopher. The learned man had been appointed as the headmaster of the school for catechumens in the Christian community. Clement replaced him after a short time, probably for a period extending over three decades, until the persecution of the emperor Septimus Severus in A.D. 202–203, which was directly promulgated against the teachers of Christian doctrines. Clement managed to escape, and he spent the rest of his life under the protection of his friend Alexander, who was bishop of a community in Cappadocia. In A.D. 215–216, the same Alexander, then bishop of Jerusalem, wrote a letter to Clement's most famous pupil Origen, his successor in Alexandria, mentioning Clement as someone who had passed away.

The *Exhortation to the Greeks*, in the Greek title *Protreptikos,* is one of Clement's earliest writings. The work is remarkable for the newness of its projected task. For the first time a Christian used the philosophical genre, created by Aristotle in the fourth century B.C. for this "exhortative" message calling for a conversion of the mind. There is nothing certain about Clement's being priest or cleric, but there is no doubt that his fiery conviction breathed a most unexpected and passionate life into the traditional genre of such exhortations.

First of all, Clement delivers a message of love. The lover is God himself; the beloved are all human beings. God's initiative consists in his self-revelation, through the divine Logos, his own Word, and through his "mouth," the Holy Spirit. Clement only alludes to these theological categories. His public could grasp them in the light of very old classical notions about the godhead, which were reactivated here on behalf of the Christian message. Clement's aim was to focus directly on the call for a personal conversion, as implied in the very mention of God's salvific action, according to his view. He introduces the theme of the divine call in naming God "a tender father" and bringing his readers back to their earliest cultural memories in learning the poems of Homer. He insists that this "calling" God, about whom he is speaking, is not just a "father" or a "master" because his revelatory teaching is "his very Word." The decisive Christianizing of this Logos, familiar to people educated in a Platonic atmosphere, counts among the lasting achievements of the Alexandrian convert in the late second and early third century. Being the "Word" of God itself, in its divine substance and also in its manifestation on earth, the call for a conversion of the mind operates with a divine power, with the transfiguring power of God's love. The Christian message, identified with the living Christ, starts by assimilating the beloved human beings to their divine lover. It possesses the unique aptitude for fulfilling all the expectations of educated Greeks, who were much more attracted to the religious mysteries in late antiquity than in earlier times. It demonstrates a perfect harmony with their longing for a kind of salvation secured by adequate knowledge. For what reason? Just because God's call in his own living Word produces "godliness."

Thus Clement never tires of celebrating the spiritual event of the divine call as experienced in a conversion to Christianity. One thinks of the theological fathers of our own century, Karl Barth and Rudolf Bultmann, hammering steadfastly upon contemporary Christian minds the principles of a decisive experience of faith. Open yourself to God's Word, and your very self will undergo a radical change. The difference with Clement is that the twentieth-century fathers identify this change as a radical crisis of all human certitudes in favor of faith, whereas Clement understood faith in response to the divine call as a rebirth of human "reason." The call recognized as the divine "Logos" captured the innermost life of the converted mind in a "logical" process, leading it out of a world demonized in helpless darkness into the radiance of Christ, "who is the sun of the Resurrection." "The light of humankind is the Word."

The shaping of biblical hermeneutics in accordance with his understanding of the principles of Christian spirituality seems to be one of Clement's major concerns according to chapter IX of his *Exhortation*. Here again his foundational initiative is similar to Barth's or Bultmann's creative steps. Could it be different? Could Christian spirituality ever renovate itself without initiating new attitudes in the reading of Scripture?

Clement describes the language of the Bible as "figuratively" meaningful: the destiny of Israel, evoked in the Bible, "prefigures" the Christ event and the Christian church. What is most important is that such a "figurative" relevance of scriptural narratives, far from speaking only to the imagination of the faithful and far from leading them into fanciful allegories, immediately implies the mysterious power of divine inspiration. From one end of Scripture to the other you read "letters which make sacred and make divine"; you cannot read them and *remain unaffected*; they are going to transform your being. Such is the dynamic efficiency of the letters contained in this sacred text, where "the mouth of the Lord" itself spells them out. The active and "informing" relevance of Scripture is "spiritual," because of the Spirit acting in it. Thus divine revelation is mediated in the most appropriate manner, as invented by God's love. "Out-spoken" by God's loving Spirit, the scriptural text becomes conformable to the ears of the beloved humankind. Received in the hearts of the believers, the same text enacts the spiritual transformation of humankind, remodeling it with the divine energies of the Word. Again, the notion of the spirituality proper to the Christian experience of faith is worked out by Clement in the realistic terms of partaking of the revealed godhead. He concludes with an image of the Word as the choirmaster of the human race, with all its members "drawn together into one love" and celebrating harmoniously, as in a "symphony," God as the "Monad," the ultimate unity of the whole redeemed cosmos.

## ATHANASIUS OF ALEXANDRIA

### *On the Interpretation of the Psalms*

Athanasius was bishop of Alexandria for 45 years, from A.D. 328 to 373. His *On the Interpretation of the Psalms* could hardly be more silent about the political history of the man who was one of the key figures among the episcopate of his time. Not only was Athanasius sent into five exiles by four successive Roman emperors, but when he was elected bishop in his own Alexandrian church he inherited a most poisoned state of affairs. On one side, an inner schism originated by Meletios, a bishop of Upper Egypt in the first years of the century, had robbed his predecessors of authority over more than half of the bishops and other clerics. This schism had been dividing the Christian communities all along the Nile Valley, as well as in the city of Alexandria itself, for a quarter of a century. On the other side, a spectacular dispute between the same predecessor of Athanasius, the old bishop Alexander, had ended in a local synod of about a hundred participants who excluded the priest Arius and his strongest Alexandrian supporters from the church. Held around A.D. 318, this synod began a controversy between the church of Alexandria and the major sees in the Orient. All of them were eager to protect Arius against a condemnation which appeared to them to be a one-sided and offensive decision made by the Alexandrian "pope." The struggle for power and for primacy among the Greek-speaking churches intensified in A.D. 324 when the emperor Constantine assumed authority in the eastern half of the empire. For the first time in its history, the Christian church could enjoy the benevolence of the supreme head of an omnipotent state administration. The era of local or universal persecutions against Christians was over. The Constantinian era opened unheard-of prospects of peace for the churches. In spite of this, their inner division and doctrinal tensions were not resolved, not even after the ruler of the empire had convoked the bishops in the spring of A.D. 325 to an imperial synod at Nicaea.

When the young Athanasius, probably not yet thirty years old, was chosen as the occupant of the most influential see among all the Christian churches at that time, the "Arian crisis" was far from being settled. Against his will, and in a political scene for which he at first looked rather unsuited, Athanasius had to act as a strong defender of his predecessor's decision, which had been confirmed at Nicaea, in excluding Arius from the church. At the same time, according to a decree of the Nicene Council, he was requested to reintegrate into the ranks of his clergy all fifteen members of the decades-long schism of Meletios. The alliance between the powerful supporters of Arius in different churches of the Orient and the Egyptian schismatic church benefited from the imperial favor of Constantius II, one of Constantine's sons, who ruled the eastern parts of the empire from A.D. 336 to 362. As a result, the Alexandrian bishop found himself involved in a series of dramatic episodes which marked his whole career. He fought a prolonged duel with Constantius, who in A.D. 351 ordered the whole epsicopacy of the western provinces to sign a decree directed against Athanasius. The emperor then "celebrated" the bishop in his most violent pamphlets and directed the secret police to catch the stubborn Alexandrian opponent in the remote hiding places of the Egyptian deserts where he was harbored in monastic communities between A.D. 356 and 362.

There is no doubt that the political hero Athanasius was as defamed as he was celebrated in his lifetime. Throughout the centuries his stereotyped image carried the mark of his troublesome and controverted ministry as a bishop. Even today, few historians attracted by his imposing figure would reach a consensus in the evaluation of such a career. It may be for that reason that not a single comprehensive biography of Athanasius has been written during the twentieth century. In taking up the challenge of contradicting the stereotyped Athanasius, one would begin reading with patience and discernment his best-known writings, such as the treatise *On the Incarnation*, his *Orations Against the Arians*, or his *Life of Anthony*. One would also need to read his lesser known works, such as the *Festal Letters* or the present letter to

Marcellinus. In such careful reading, the surprising fact begins to emerge that even in the more polemic *Apologies*, Athanasius is revealed as a pastor, much less interested in imperial politics than in the religious and spiritual education of his flock. If correctly noted, this primary concern reveals in all the Athanasian treatises and letters a vivid interest in the Bible and its use in a pastoral pedagogy.

As an inspired interpreter of Scripture, Athanasius has not transmitted in his literary legacy a single commentary on a book of the Old or New Testament. He never considered himself a professional exegete of sacred Scripture. This is in sharp contrast with Origen, who had taught Christian doctrine in Alexandria about a century earlier. Origen (A.D. 185–253/54) had built up a vast synthesis of theological insights, resting on a learned assumption of philosophical principles which he had inherited from the Middle-Platonic culture of his time. Origen's thinking was impregnated with the spirituality proper to Alexandrian Gnosticism. For the most part, his impressive message took the form of scriptural commentaries. The Bible and the interpretation of the Bible was for Origen the most appropriate reference to communicate his thoughts to the Christian community. He became a world-famous theologian who was an authentic genius in his own right, and he succeeded in fixing the techniques of interpreting Scripture for many centuries to come. Though it was his custom to keep secret the systematic principles of his understanding of Christianity, he was all the more open to emphasizing the recognized values of a spiritual interpretation of the Bible.

When Athanasius took up his responsibilities as leader in matters of doctrine, the experience of the Alexandrian church community was completely transformed. His style of leadership, invested with a personal, teaching charism, was no longer exercised at the intellectual level of contemporary academics. Nor would he show a concern for bridging the gap between the non-Christian culture of his time and the inner life of the church. Thus, he was not employing the language of apologetics, nor did he experience the need to emulate Origen's incomparable accomplishment of harmonizing by his own intellectual capacity the main trends of Greek culture with the religious expectations proper to his local church. From the outset, Athanasius's task in the treatise *On the Incarnation* was to give a voice to the silent majority in his believing community. He never felt a real concern for the abstract speculations of intellectuals. Even if they were eager to introduce a new systematic strength into the public predication of the gospel, the young bishop saw them more or less withdrawn to the fringe of this community. Perhaps he was mistaken. The history of Christian thought would have followed a different course had he thought otherwise, but Athanasius could no longer conceive of the reality of the church in the old fashioned and highly Origenian categories of an intellectual elite, hierarchically paralleled to the bishop's office, and a lower level of the "simple" believers, the so-called illiterates. Arius, on the other hand, was still inclined to these gnostic-type categories. He expressed this attitude best in the prologue of his pamphlet *Thalia*. The literary remains of his true disciples, while witnessing a high degree of a legitimate theological awareness, are consonant with this viewpoint. There are also a few good reasons for agreeing with their doctrinal task in the years after the "great persecution" of Diocletian and on the doorstep of the Constantian era. Without any noticeable intellectual revival, except the Arian movement, the Alexandrian church between A.D. 315 and 325 underwent quick and dramatic changes. The first post-Nicene bishop of Alexandria, consecrated in A.D. 328, had matured precisely through these changes. He was by no means bound to the more intellectualistic foundations of the Alexandrian church proper to its school tradition of the third century. Athanasius belonged to a new generation, the post-Diocletian era, beyond the watershed dividing his generation and that of his predecessor Alexander and of Arius himself.

The basic evidence of Athanasian spirituality claims that the divine revelation, communicated by Scripture, is given to all the faithful in common and at once, and is mediated for them by the church itself by its rites, its sacraments, and its true openness to the gospel message. In other words, the actual church community acts as a living interpretation of the divine mysteries contained in Scripture. In this regard, Athanasius never made a special case for the hierarchical ministry in the church. He saw the church as instrumental for everyone's access to the complete truth of Scripture. The sacramental and communitarian experience of faith, which is the essential church life, actualizes the very reality of salvation fulfilled in Christ. This actualizing process invades the whole social up-growing of the church. It also yields answers to the questions of individual Christians, questions expressed by them on the level of their common Christian experience. Therefore, Athanasius called his fellow believers to verify the actual truth of Scripture as assumed by them in becoming members of the church. This call may, by given circumstances, insist on the vital Christian certitudes shared in a traditional catechesis, as in *On the Incarnation*, or it may claim a more polemic form of orthodoxy, as in the *Orations Against the Arians*. It always remains centered on an incarnational vision of the mystery of salvation experienced here and now in the church. Scripture has been taken out of the hands of learned experts and given to the people. Thus the reason Athanasius did not repeat the scholarly initiatives of former teachers and leaders in his church by producing his own contributions to biblical exegesis becomes clearer. For him such an exegesis resulted in a less tireless celebration of the actual experience of Christian faith. His way of interpreting the Bible was to link it with the current debates in his community and with the daily existence of its members. In the form of a narrative pedagogy, he discussed the debated issues with biblical arguments always oriented toward the central beliefs of the church. His way of reasoning always remained accessible to the man in the street. To bishops, to ordinary lay people, and to monks as well, Athanasius repeatedly offered a doctrinal synthesis born of his lifelong meditation of Scripture. This synthesis focused on the paschal mystery of Christ actualized in the faithful experience of individuals and in the church as such. The present experience, with its private and its public dimensions, found in Christ its ultimate truth, and this truth identified everyone's experience in the narratives of all the Scriptures. Certainly it would be a challenging, yet a truly rewarding enterprise to observe how Athanasius worked out his central biblical intuitions in his various writings, dated from his first *Festal Letters* circa A.D. 330 to the last one in 371. This letter to Marcellinus makes no exception in the line of pastoral literature.

*On the Interpretation of the Psalms* is a private answer sent to a friend who was recovering from sickness. As was frequently the custom in antiquity, the private letter was meant to be read in a public circle among relatives and friends. Marcellinus had applied the forced leisure of his convalescence to an intense reading of Scripture, mainly the Book of Psalms. Thus we are introduced into the spiritual world of earnest people using their free time to improve their religious education. This was fashionable and commonplace among the upper class in late antiquity. Nothing in this letter to Marcellinus suggests that Marcellinus held any kind of ecclesiastical office. He was certainly not a monk; Athanasius would have addressed him as such. The letter does not include the slightest allusion to a monastic way of life, and Athanasius would hardly have complimented a monk for having employed his convalescence in becoming more familiar with the Psalms. Monks recited psalms from the first day of their reclusion in the desert.

The letter is carefully written in a peaceful tone, with the obvious purpose of communicating the best of Athanasius's own experience as a reader of psalms. The goal of the letter, as announced in no. 1, is to share with Marcellinus "the task of trying to grasp the inner meaning of every single psalm." Since such a task could be entered upon in many different ways, we should suppose that the letter shows the way of interpreting the psalms in conformity to Athanasius's own practice. The literary convention of the "old man" dispenses the writer of the letter from speaking in his own name. Athanasius employs that convention by framing the letter with a literary inclusion, repeating his mention of the old man in the last paragraph of the letter, no. 33. In no. 2, the old man is supposed to address Athanasius as "my child," when he starts telling him the content of the present letter; "my child" comes back in no. 30. Having started his long talk with an enthusiastic statement, "The Book of Psalms, like a blessed garden bearing many different fruits, contains the themes of the other books . . . ," the "old" mediator of inspired knowledge recapitulates his teaching in the same no. 30, admonishing his "child" to read the Book "and then select from it, as from the fruits of a blessed garden, what is useful. . . ." In fact, there is more than a simple farming image in this comparison. Athanasius intends to describe the Psalter as the quintessence of the whole Scripture, and he also finds in this Scripture, actualized in the experience of faith, the quintessence of true church life. As he insists elsewhere, the salvific reality of the church is like a new "paradise," meaning a baptismal actualizing of the original paradise, revealed in Genesis 2. The artistic frame of the letter underlines its mystical core, as is often the case in Athanasian writings.

The main divisions of the letter lead to similar observations. A first section, running from no. 2 to no. 8, invites one to consider what the Psalter has in common with the rest of Scripture. Again the framing procedure indicates the central purpose of this section. As no. 2 states that "the Book of Psalms . . . contains the themes of the other books," the final paragraph of the section (no. 8) concludes with: "Everything, then, which is sung in the Psalms is also proclaimed in each of the other books." But what is "sung in the Psalms" and also proclaimed in the rest of Scripture is nothing other than the mystery of the salvific incarnation of God, as *deployed* in the gospel narratives. This first part of *On the Interpretation of the Psalms* comes very close to the structural and doctrinal characteristics of the treatise *On the Incarnation* and of the first two *Orations Against the Arians*.

The second section reintroduces "the old man" of the prologue of the letter and announces its third and last occurrence in the conclusion. This section runs from no. 9 to no. 14 with the intention of giving a global survey of what is distinctive in the Book of Psalms. In a first step, the "old man" underlines the paradox "that what is proclaimed is the one and the same symphony of the Spirit" through and through in all Scriptures (no. 9); then, in concluding no. 9, he moves to a second phase, which consists of recognizing the distinctiveness of the Book of Psalms from an artistic and literary point of view. It "has the special characteristic of communicating in song what is detailed in prose in other books." This remark opens immediately a hermeneutical perspective. Being "songs," the Psalms need to be interpreted as such: their "melody" conditions their proper "treatment" of the topics which they share with other books of the Bible. In the same way, in the second *Oration Against the Arians*, Athanasius had begun his famous discussion of Prov. 8:22 by calling for special attention to be given to the "proverbial" genre of biblical statements. Even more interesting is the concentrated teaching about the Spirit in this second section. Having focused in the first section on the sort of narrative Christology which one finds also in his treatise *On the Incarnation* (c. A.D. 335) and in the first two *Orations Against the Arians* (A.D. 339), Athanasius reminds his friend in the second section about his other letters, *Concerning the Holy Spirit* (c. A.D. 359), which he wrote to the closest of all his friends, the bishop Serapion. Thanks to the form of "songs" given by him to the Psalms, the Spirit infuses into them "an exceptional quality of perceptiveness," so that the faithful can contemplate in the Psalms "the movements of his [or her] own soul" (no. 10). After having partially illustrated this point with a few examples of psalms linked with afflictions, or thanksgiving, or persecution, or praise, the "old man," alias Athanasius, opens no. 11 with one of his inveterate rhetorical tricks: "In addition, there is a further paradox in the Psalms." Always aware of his reader's reception of the instruction, Athanasius is concerned to provide every pedagogical help in following the text. He employs the devices of transitions, of short recapitulations, of literary inclusions, and of clearly distinguished steps in the gradual analysis of a continuous theme. When the author comes to the end of no. 11, he summarizes his argument in the most natural way: "The paradox of the Psalms is that . . . each person sings what has been written as about himself or herself." The meaning of such a personal appropriation of the psalmic message for Athanasius becomes clear in nos. 12–13. The words used by the Spirit in the Psalms operate like a mirror in the reader's soul. As Christians reach a level of self-understanding inspired by Scripture, they actualize Scripture in the process of the actual economy of salvation in which they are immersed. What the Spirit had sung in Psalms was "said about us"; the psalmic words had "been expressed . . . for us as models and patterns" (no. 12). The anticipatory "models" become fulfilled reality in our experience of faith, and this experience of ours finds its true "voice" in order to identify and to express itself, namely, "the voice in the psalms" (no. 13), which lets us discover that we are really taught by Christ himself: "Before he came among us, he taught us by the sound of a voice." The same characteristic shift from focusing on anonymous subjects, individual data, to the pastoral "us," so central in the first two *Orations Against the Arians*, introduces here in no. 13 a remarkable christological setting. As all the Psalms had been sung about us (no. 12), so has the Savior accomplished his salvific incarnation "for our sake" in order "to show us" himself as a "model" or an "image" (no. 13). This supernatural "imaging," sketched in the terms of the Christian Platonism which provided the basic theological language common to Athanasius and Marcellinus, is seen as a transforming endeavor. For Christ himself "not only taught, but he performed what he taught." He did this "for us," for whom the Psalms secure "the remedy and the means of amendment of every movement of the soul" (no. 13).

One could hardly imagine a more substantial reminder of Athanasius's theological anthropology than what is recalled by him in no. 12 and no. 13 in *On the Interpretation of the Psalms*.

It would be worth looking here for more explicit parallels with *On the Incarnation*, even with *Against the Heathen*, and also with *Orations Against the Arians* I–II and with the *Letters to Serapion*.

The third section runs from no. 15 to no. 31, nos. 32–33 adding a general conclusion. Finally, in this last section, the direct response to Marcellinus's attempt "to grasp the inner meaning of every single psalm" (prologue, no. 1) is offered. For only now can this "inner meaning" be correctly defined in the terms of the Athanasian vision of an incarnational salvation. What is "inner" in the words of the Psalms is also, most precisely, "inner" in ourselves, who read the Psalms in the church. It is our own "soul" exposed in faith to the inspired action of the psalmic Spirit. As in all his authentic writings, Athanasius tends to assimilate biblical exegesis with pastoral dogmatics. There is also a constant feature of his creative authority as a theologian at work here: he never tires of plunging with new insights into the actualized mystery of Christ, which is identical with day-to-day Christian existence in its deepest relevance. As he says in the introduction of his amazing survey of each of the 150 psalms collected in the book: "the Book of the Psalms possesses an image of the way in which souls course through life," and this "image" is "the way of life of the Savior in the body" (no. 14). Such a concrete spirituality with its christological focus represents the proper contribution of Athanasius to the Alexandrian tradition, and his mystical legacy to all the churches in the classical Christianity of east and west.

The analytic survey of the 150 psalms starts as a matter of fact in no. 14, with a first set of psalmic sequences organized with respect to the *literary* form of the biblical songs: some are composed in a "narrative form," others produce a "form of a confession," or "of admonition," and so forth, and there are "special hymn forms." The same pattern of literary composition had already been applied at the beginning of this second section, where Athanasius had intended to underline the *global* distinctiveness of the Book of Psalms as he had noted earlier about the "song" form of the Psalms, before going on to claim that their main themes were focusing on the movements of the human soul. Here, before starting the third section and in introducing it, he insists again on the literary factor ("the Psalms are composed in such a way that . . ." [no. 15]), before devoting his attention to each *single* psalm. It would be intriguing to observe in some detail how Athanasius organized such a venture. He mentions explicitly the Psalms in their numerical order, from Psalm 1 (no. 15) to Psalm 150 (no. 26), but his procedure is much more complex and seems to reflect the themes he had earlier announced. In any case, such a piece of spiritual hermeneutics, rich in christological overtones but in an immediate reference to "the practices of the spiritual life" (no. 1), is a unique treasure unparalleled in the literature of the patristic era.

The third section adds a few practical directions, which are primarily linked with what has been stated above concerning the literary features of the Psalms: "it is very necessary not to pass over the reasons why words of this kind are to be intoned with melody and song" (no. 27). The "reasons" developed are very similar, in their conception and even in their verbal style, to the rational conveniences of the divine incarnation, deployed by Athanasius in *On the Incarnation* or elsewhere. Witnessing the Alexandrian mysticism already encountered in Clement of Alexandria's *Exhortation,* Athanasius echoes a classical motif in comparing the harmonious music of a harp with the spiritual being of a human person "attentive to the Spirit" (no. 28).

"Say and sing what is written without artifice of any kind—just as it was expressed—so that the righteous men who gave them to us will recognize them as their own and will pray with us" (no. 31). It is in regard to "us," the pastoral community which was the usual horizon of Athanasian theology, that the author of the letter evokes for the last time the actualizing process which has given him a decisive hermeneutical key for his interpretation of the Psalms. As the will of the Spirit had created the form of "songs" for our spiritual convenience, so are "we" who are now in the church ordered to articulate the Psalms "without artifice," so that the psalmists from an old past may "pray with us" in the unity of an identical, unique economy of salvation.

Over a century later, when this letter to Marcellinus, or reports about it, had reached Augustine, the new bishop of Hippo remembered the final advice of Athanasius (*Confessions* IX, 4). Ambrose before him, and Cassiodorus in the sixth century, would also take great advantage of this letter *On the Interpretation of the Psalms*. It is still to be determined how far it inspired generations of believers through the centuries, one of its latest authoritative roles being a key reference in the Apostolic Constitution of Pope Pius X, on the use of the Psalter in the Roman breviary, in November 1911.

## GREGORY OF NAZIANZUS

### Sermon 38

In the generation after Athanasius, a small group of relatives and friends known as the Cappadocian fathers played a spectacular role in the Christian church's spread through modern Turkey. Their mothers and sisters had, more than once, a decisive influence on their choices. The family saga began at the turn of the third century with the conversion of Macrina the Elder by Gregory the Wonderworker, a former disciple of Origen, who became a bishop of his hometown on the southern border of the Black Sea. After two generations of fervent Christian family life, Basil, one of the grandchildren of Macrina, was deeply impressed by his sister Macrina the Younger and by the religious community of women which she had built up around herself. Still a layman and a bachelor after five years of academic training in Athens where he had met Gregory, the future bishop of Nazianzus, Basil began working on the earliest draft of what would be known later on as his monastic rules. He retired deep into the countryside in a place called Annisi with his friend Gregory. Shortly afterward, Basil was elected bishop of Caesarea in Cappadocia and became undisputedly the episcopal leader of the whole of the Christianity in the Roman Orient until his death in A.D. 379 at the age of forty-nine. A firm character, he laid down the institutional basis for oriental Christian monasticism and championed the Nicene orthodoxy against the pro-Arian politics of Emperor Valens by nominating his own candidates to different episcopal sees in his area. One of them was his younger brother Greogry whom he pressured into accepting the episcopal office after the death of his wife Theosibia, and who gave lasting fame to the small see of Nyssa. Another of Basil's candidates was, of course, his close friend Gregory, whom he appointed in A.D. 372 to an insignificant place called Sasima. Poor Gregory, a poet and a mystic, after describing his new see as utterly despicable in a letter he sent to Basil, vanished into the wilderness of Isauria for at least four years. After that period of asceticism and pure contemplation, Gregory became the pastor of the small Nicene community of

Constantinople in the spring of A.D. 379. About a year later, solicited by the new emperor, Theodosius, who had declared himself in favor of Nicaea, Gregory moved from his chapel to the cathedral of the capital. He played a very important part in the imperial synod of A.D. 381, convoked by Theodosius in Constantinople with the purpose of putting a definitive conclusion to the Arian dispute. In his homily for Pentecost A.D. 379, Gregory had dared, in an unprecedented statement from the pulpit, to honor the Holy Spirit in naming it "God," despite the absence of this explicit title in Scripture. In a series of famous sermons delivered in the chapel of the Anastasia, before the council was held, he had also expounded a profound synthesis of Trinitarian doctrine. By A.D. 381, disgusted with ecclesiastical summits and politics, he retired once more from society, this time into the vast domain of his rich family, where he spent the last decade of his life in productive leisure, "enlivened" with severe daily asceticism. During his retirement he wrote as many as 400 poems that we know of; he published the first collection of private letters put on the market by a Christian. He introduced autobiography among the genres of Christian literature: the poem he wrote *On His Life*, totalled as many as 1949 verses, a rhetorical and sometimes touching description of the inner life of his soul. A son of aristocratic Cappadocian landowners, a brilliant speaker, well-educated and versed in philosophy, Gregory exemplifies, as a contemporary of Ambrose of Milan and just prior to Augustine in North Africa, the attractiveness of the Christian doctrine among the wealthy upper class, and moreso he incarnates the Christian ideal among the men trained in the best universities of his time.

In Sermon 38, *On the Nativity of the Savior*, in words that are crystal clear, Gregory of Nazianzus does not hesitate to launch out into the heightened language of poetry. Nor did he hesitate in this rather formal address to employ the richest concentration of biblical symbols and theological insights. One may suppose his congregation was not more qualified than any other for the reception of a homily of such refinement and polish, but the stylish and evocative notations of Gregory's contemplation speak for themselves. They transcend the local setting and constitute for all times a perfect example of highly educated mysticism practiced by a bishop in his pulpit. Listeners of today, if sufficiently attuned to the scriptural nuances, would no less enjoy Gregory's doctrinal rigor and clarity than did the auditors of the late fourth century. The first two paragraphs of the homily, translated and edited in this collection, open with a vision of the celebration of the liturgical mystery, while the final two paragraphs invite the auditors to envisage their personal and faithful response to such a mystery.

In no. 1, the cosmic significance of Christ's coming in the flesh fills heaven and earth with joy. For many centuries, religion and spirituality in various Greek traditions had focused on the cosmos as being the ultimate realm of divine revelation. Here we receive the Christian version of this ancient and pervasive religiosity, which was deeply rooted in Hellenistic minds. The final rhetorical question of no. 1, "Who would not give praise to him who is the end of all?" acts as a prelude to the more historical theme of no. 2, which also leads to the same "end of all": "when he comes from the heavens taking his seat as judge."

In no. 2, the divine incarnation is acclaimed as an event overarching all times, to which the liturgy offers a mystical access. If this event is at first celebrated as a "light" and as "a great light of knowledge," it is because the homily belongs to the feast of the Epiphany on January 6, not to our western Christmas of December 25. As in a baptismal predication, Gregory here associated "light" with "newness." The reference to 2 Cor. 5:7 recalls the cosmic horizon stretched out in no. 1: "All things have been made new." The opposition between "letter" and "Spirit," or "shadows" and "truth," prepares the listener for the rather obscure—at least for us, if not for Gregory's congregation—allusion to the double nature of Christ, whom he compared with Melchizedek, as Christ is "without a mother" when generated as Son of God by the Father, and "without a father" when born from the virgin Mary. Again Gregory refers to the cosmic relevance of the divine incarnation. "Cosmos above" means the "spiritual" or the "noetic" cosmos, the world beyond the firmament and the planets, where divine beings, such as angels and archangels, celebrate a celestial liturgy. The mythical and theological themes linked with the "cosmos above" were numerous and amazingly vivid throughout antiquity. They entered into Christian translations with their philosophical overtones mainly through the synthesis of Origen. The Cappadocian fathers were the promoters of an Origenian revival through their own theological writings. Even when they rejected Origen's systematic presuppositions in fundamental issues, such as the thesis of a preexistence of human souls in God's cosmos before their earthly life, they nevertheless intensified the links between Origen's mysticism and such cosmological categories.

The events celebrated in the homily need to be adequately recognized in a biblical setting, according to the traditional Christian understanding of prophecies, repeated by the liturgy itself. "Christ" is the one who "urges us" in the liturgical Scripture readings. But in the same way Gregory had limited himself just two lines before to a quite mysterious allusion to "the cosmos above," so does he select here only a very few prophetic phrases. "All you nations" announces the successful spread of Christianity through the provinces and even through the higher social levels in the Constantinian empire; "sovereignty" introduces the glory of the paschal mystery of Christ into the contemplation of his birth; the prophetic title "Mighty Counsellor" allows a glance at the Son's being in the inner-Trinitarian life of God. The other title "angel" links the vision of the immanent Trinity with the economy of salvation, for which the Son had been sent as an envoy and as interpreter of divine mysteries. The reference to John the Baptist's ministry provides an appropriate transition from the prophets of Israel to the Christian preacher's own message. Origen had made much of this same transition in his commentaries on the figure of John.

With a liturgical "I," Gregory begins his own response to the event of the "Theophany" or "Manifestation of God" celebrated in the liturgy. Immediately he drops back into the cosmic frame, which obviously speaks most spontaneously to his own spirituality. The "power of the day" is the dynamic inbreaking of God's "truth," which was already described as abrogating the laws of nature. Then, until "Jesus Christ" is named and identified according to Heb. 13:8, Gregory continues to develop the Christianized notion of the godhead inherited from the philosophical Greek monotheism, which was much older than the church itself. It is our responsibility today to react with critical awareness in regard to such a basic notion, foundational in Western civilization. For millennia, Western religious traditions have been shifting from the basis on which these metaphysical categories of the godhead were resting. It is now the duty of modern interpreters to examine how such a category was vital for Christian spirituality in the patristic church, and what its significance is today. Gregory's short propositions outline the whole *theo*-logical approach to the divine incarnation in the ancient church, as a "high" Christology in defense of the classical *theos* assimilated to the Trinity of the Christian predication. This *theos* is by itself an immaterial logos; "invisible," which also meant unknowable in a proper way; "impalpable," which underscores a degree of absolute transcendency. Finally, this *theos* needed to be confessed as "timeless," for there were always ongoing debates dedicated in the major schools of philosophy to the notions of time and eternity assumed in theology. In a discreetly anti-Arian turn, Gregory makes a clear distinction between the timeless Son of God and the "time-ly" incarnate Son of Man.

At this point there is a certain polemical turn in the argument. In stereotyped language he brings the sublime doctrine of the incarnation back to earth, where the church, as Gregory sees it, struggles for its ultimate recognition by Jews, Greeks, and heretics. It seems quite obvious that the mention of the last day is introduced here like another kind of stereotype, unreflective of the spiritual experience of the speaker. But once more the cosmic dimension intervenes, the dimension most vivid in the religious cultural background of the sermon, and enriches the liturgical sense for the celebrated event. Without a mention of Christ's ascension, Gregory's homily on the birth of the Savior would have lacked an essential aspect of the incarnational economy of salvation contemplated in its global unity. This reference, like the liturgical celebration of the ascension itself at that time, brings to mind the ultimate coming of Christ. Thus, "the heavens" remain a familiar part of the new religious cosmos pervaded by the universal relevance of the salvation economy centered in Christ.

In the final part of the homily, no. 17 and no. 18, Gregory exhorts his auditors to take an active part in the celebration of the nativity of their Savior. The way in which he suggests the active response he is expecting from them reveals his understanding of the essential features of a spiritual way of life. Gregory's congregation is expected to conduct themselves in such a way that they reproduce in their own lives biblical models. The Hellenistic culture may have molded through and through the mind of an educated man like Gregory; nevertheless, this preacher measured virtue only with paradigms taken from Scripture. In fact, all the details of the gospel narratives which are related from the birth of Christ onwards are integrated into his call for ethical improvement. He calls to mind the narratives of Scripture first of all because they allow him to formulate his demands in the most persuasive terms. Once again, we notice that the basic pattern of a given spirituality, as expressed in the texts collected here, derives from a specific way of interpreting Scripture.

The main attitudes to which the auditors are exhorted reveal also Gregory's notion of spirituality. They are contemplative joy and reverence, growth in being "logical" thanks to the nourishment of the "Logos" (the Word), self-offering, and praise. If adopted as their own, such attitudes would introduce the listeners into the mystery of the liturgy they are celebrating. As he has argued from the beginning of the homily, Gregory reiterates his conviction that such a mystery would establish a communication between the earthly congregation now addressed by him and the heavenly one, the "angels" and "the choir of the archangels." Thus we are brought back in a lyrical finale to "the cosmos above." Gregory concludes his homily, in no. 18, on this note in describing the earthly anticipation of celestial "festivities" as true discipleship of Christ. He expands the Pauline motif of imitating Christ, already noted in *The Martyrs of Lyon*, with an imaginative artistry, appealing to a people who no longer considered themselves as called to martyrdom. The gospel narratives about Jesus, from his birth on, are vividly recalled and applied to the present auditors in a vibrant exhortation. As in his reference to the prophets in no. 2, Gregory is eager again, in these final series of images, to link the celebration of Christ's birth with a special thought for his paschal mystery: "Suffer to be stoned. . . . Taste the gall. . . . Finally allow yourself to be crucified. . . ." In an authentic Pauline tone, he goes over to the doxology which concludes the sermon.

## AMBROSE OF MILAN

### Concerning Virgins

When Ambrose wrote his apology *Concerning Virgins* he was almost forty-three years old. It was written in the form of a letter addressed to his older sister Marcellina who had always impressed him by her strict piety. She had followed the path of a heroine among their Christian ancestors, a grandaunt who had been martyred. Her own sacrifice would be of a different sort, the spiritual self-immolation replacing the bloody death. In about A.D. 352, when Ambrose was at most eighteen years old, Marcellina was consecrated a virgin in the Vatican basilica by the Roman bishop Liberius. At that time, political pressure and inner tensions severely disturbed the Roman church. People were still wondering, a quarter of a century after Nicaea, if they had to choose between the Nicene orthodoxy and the religious politics of the emperor. The Arian crisis gave no rest to Liberius. Kidnapped by night and forced to meet the emperor in his headquarters, he suffered a temporary exile before subscribing to a compromising paper which allowed him to return to Rome.

Whereas Marcellina turned her back on the ecclesiastical turmoil, following with her companions the call to monasticism, Ambrose was busy with his classical and juridical studies. While formally enrolled as a catechumen, he remained true to his Christian family heritage but did not become involved in any theological dispute. His training prepared him for public service. His taste inclined him to prefer the Greek authors, old poets, and classical historians, as well as more recent authors. Of course, he knew Virgil and Cicero by heart. A son of wealthy landowners, eager to assimilate the humanistic traditions patronized by the Neoplatonic philosophers of his time, Ambrose is seen as one of the last Romans gifted with complete acquaintance with Greek culture. At the age of thirty-six, he was named governor of the province of Aemilia-Liguria in northern Italy. His new residence was in Milan. His role was that of a judge in the service of the city. Among the different factions in need of a local arbiter, the Christians certainly proved to be no exception. In the spring of A.D. 374, their main church so vibrated with resounding rhetoric that the governor felt the need to introduce some calm into their arguments. As they strove to decide on the election of a new bishop, they turned their attention to Ambrose and, surely by divine inspiration, acclaimed him as their providential candidate. A man only five feet, four inches tall, but a born leader, Ambrose could not escape God's call. He tried to flee and hide in the countryside. His sister Marcellina's luminous path seemed to legitimate for him a quest for contemplation and asceticism in the wilderness. But in November of A.D. 374 he was baptized, and a short week later without any respite he found himself consecrated as a bishop.

His first spiritual essay some three years later was dedicated to Marcellina. It is the apology *Concerning Virgins*. Before considering their immediate concern, these pages deserve to be recognized as a striking illustration of what spirituality really meant for

Ambrose. First, it meant a deeply personal endeavor of assimilating Scripture. In the free and silent hours of the night, the newly elected bishop of Milan had distilled into his inmost soul the message of the Bible. In *Concerning Virgins* the books of divine revelation appear at once to be the only literary authorities acknowledged by the highly educated convert. Second, "our gift of speech," as the author of the essay puts it, is nothing other than "the eloquence of God entrusted to us" (no. 1). Spirituality, in Christian terms, communicates a social message characterized by divine persuasiveness. It embodies all that each section of society needs to know about Christ. One of the most appropriate forms for such a communication is provided by books. They exclude the boasting common to orators, mainly in the oratorical institutions of late antiquity: "A book does not blush," he reminds us in the words of Cicero (no. 1). Third, as indicated already, Christian spirituality is directed toward a metamorphosis of society. In *Concerning Virgins*, Ambrose intends to question with a fearless lucidity the basic structures of the Roman patriarchal family life. His clear intention is to introduce freedom for spiritual choice into the sacred realm of the traditional bonds linked together by the paterfamilias. The whole apology illustrates this purpose.

Thus the model of a sacralized virginity, exemplified in his own family by a beloved sister, became for Ambrose a burning issue. In pleading in its favor, the young bishop does not seem to consider the monastic institutions as such; rather, he emphasizes the mystical and social challenges of the individuals. As a true founder of a lasting tradition in the Christian West, Ambrose approaches all the existential problems linked with sacralized virginity in *Concerning Virgins*. His approach is a mixture of deeply held biblical convictions, of a juridical logic firmly molded in attractive literary forms and, last but not least, a spiritual poetry inspired by the most exquisite and mature judgment in psychological matters. Far from introducing a world-denying and dualistic view of Scripture, this advocate of female virginity celebrates openly this specific dimension of liberation initiated in his society by its response to the gospel message.

In what he calls his "eulogy" of consecrated virgins, Ambrose begins with considerable circumspection. A sound dose of shrewdness, sprinkled with vibrant touches of humor, pervades his artistically written prose. He immediately announces the final goal he is envisaging: "I shall proclaim the family of the Lord, for

27

the immaculate Lord has consecrated for himself an immaculate family even out of this body full of human frailty" (no. 4). Thus, it is truly the sacred structures of the traditional Roman family he has chosen as his target in the scope of this short essay. But far from launching a frontal attack against such a venerated institution, Ambrose begins with the popular and familiar praise of martyrdom. Again he does not hide his ultimate purpose: "I shall call upon the martyr, I shall proclaim the virgin" (no. 6). The reason for his detour, he says, is that a martyr's title is publicly praised, whereas virginity is a "title of modesty." The celebrated martyr is Agnes, mentioned by name in no. 5 and no. 19, thus providing the frame for the first part of Ambrose's treatise. The initial sequence (nos. 5–9) begins with a sagacious description of the martyr's behavior as inspired by the ideal of virginity: "No band could enclose such tender limbs" (no. 7). "A bride would not hasten to the marriage bed with as joyful step as the virgin went forward to the place of punishment . . . , the cup of life barely tasted . . ." (no. 8). "What promises of marriage were advanced!" (no. 9). The sequence concludes in pointing out that in Agnes's case one could observe "in the one victim, a double martyrdom. . . . She remains a virgin and obtains martyrdom" (no. 9). A second sequence (nos. 10–19) justifies from there on the new ecclesiastical title of virgin, linked with the well-recognized title of martyr. In a first step (nos. 10–13), Ambrose introduces the *biblical* support for such a title. Not only does virginity come from heaven with Christ's birth (no. 11) but it also summarizes all the attributes of the church's mystery, as foretold in the ancient Scriptures (no. 12). Ambrose takes care to quote the Scripture already so familiar to his readers through liturgical readings of the New Testament. With a strict sense for juridical statements, he concludes this step in noting: "Therefore we have the authority of ancient times and the fullness of the declaration in Christ" (no. 13). The figurative truth of consecrated virgins in the church derives from both Testaments. It rests directly on the christological core of the church's teaching.

A second step (nos. 14–19) adds the most convenient *apologetical* proofs in favor of ecclesiastical virginity. There is a gradation noticeable in the series of these proofs, a sort of ascending scale of arguments, leading to a clearer recognition of the transcendent superiority of Christian virgins. First, in Ambrose's sharp estimate, the vestal virgins are stripped of their title because their virginity is not permanent. In such a case, he argues, "temporary" implies a basic "corruption," as it "bids young girls to modesty and old women to wantonness." His rhetorics tend to adopt a more sarcastic stance: "What mystery! What words!" (no. 15). Then he mentions another commonplace in early Christian apologetics: the Phrygian rites and the orgies of Bacchus (no. 16). Finally, his irony culminates in the story of "a certain Pythagorean virgin" popularized through satirical pamphlets against the old-fashioned philosophical schools, and smuggled into Christian literature before Ambrose. What the latter adds is a ferocious outcry of his own disgust: "an example of speechlessness but a lax discharge of chastity" (no. 18). The obvious conclusion of the apologetical argument is underlined in no. 19, with a final reference to Agnes completing the first part of the apology.

The second part of *Concerning Virgins* runs from no. 20 to no. 39. Again the reader is alerted by the same inner disposition noted in the first part. The first sequence (nos. 20–24) is biblical, as in nos. 10–13. Here again, the two central motives of the Ambrosian notion of virginity are played out together: Christ, as the primary source of Christian virginity, in no. 21; the church, as the perfect symbol and actual realization of Christian virginity, in no. 22. It is in this substantial frame of biblical thought that Ambrose locates the discussion about the virgins of today. At first, he limits himself to quoting insistently 1 Cor. 7 (nos. 23–24), which offers him at the same time a transition to the apologetical sequence of his second section (nos. 25–29). Closely following 1 Cor. 7, several famous arguments against the condition of married people find an echo in this portion of Ambrose's apology. The satirical literature on this issue had been flourishing for centuries in both the Greek and Latin literature of late antiquity. Shortly before Ambrose wrote *Concerning Virgins*, the topic had made a spectacular entry into Christian writings in the treatise *On Virginity*, published by Gregory of Nyssa. A comparison with the present apology illuminates the sober tact of the Milanese bishop, himself never married, in contrast with his widowed colleague from Cappadocia.

The third sequence of Part II (nos. 30–39) may best be evaluated as a theological synthesis which recapitulates the notion of virginity stated in the former sequences of this same part. First, the virgins, now addressed in a direct speech ("you, blessed virgins"), are invited to seek in God alone the meaning of their existence (no. 30). They are at once confronted with the virginal mystery of "the holy church . . . filled by the Spirit, not by a husband" (no. 31). They are acclaimed as a divine gift, redeeming their own parents and keeping them free of all the concerns associated with the married status of a daughter (no. 32).

More forcefully than in no. 24, where this theme had only been announced, in no. 34 Ambrose refutes the objection of parents who may claim that he denigrates marriage itself. Finally, he concludes this third sequence with asserting once more the divine superiority of Christian virginity (no. 35). Christ is identified with the bridegroom of the Song of Solomon (no. 36). The "beauty of the virginal body" is "consecrated by the Holy Spirit" (no. 37). The "perfume" and "the flower of virginal chastity" remind the whole church of the paschal mystery of Christ (no. 39). Here, the highly allusive style of Ambrose's theological meditation strains its limits as he intensifies the concentration of images and phrases from Scripture (no. 39), anticipating the last theological sequence of the treatise in its third part.

The third part (nos. 40–53) includes a pastoral exhortation already signaled in no. 39: "See what a course is assigned to you, virgin," and is punctuated by paternal addresses like: "Daughter, how I wish you . . . " or "Imitate it, daughter" (no. 41), or again "Virgin, take . . . " (no. 44), and "forearm yourself, virgin . . . " (no. 46), always in the singular, and all through the formal exhortation (nos. 40–46). In no. 46 Ambrose's thought slips over again into a more theological contemplation of the christological motifs always integrated with his teaching on sacralized virginity. They include a vivid reference to the mystery of the church (no. 47), and even an explicit statement of Trinitarian or Nicene theology (no. 48). Ambrose ends his parenesis, or formal exhortation, with a glowing assurance given of the "holy virgins" (nos. 49–50): "But for you, holy virgins, there is a special protection" (no. 51), namely the protection of God's angels. It is significant that such a comforting vision leads him to speak of the final resurrection from the dead (no. 52), in accord with a presentation for Christian doctrine within the traditional catechesis of the economy of salvation. In reference to the Old Testament, Ambrose does not miss a last opportunity to exercise his rhetorical skills with a pointed witticism. Concerning old Noah, he dryly observes "he whom the flood could not denude, was made nude by wine!" (no. 53).

Additional remarks, not secondary ones, are to be found in nos. 54 through 65. At the start of no. 54, "a further point," disconnected from what precedes it in the apology, invites the "sister" (Marcellina?) to reject any desire to please, be it in her person (no. 54), or with her ears and her neck (no. 55), or wealth (no. 56). Then a last section from no. 57 to no. 61 discusses the local situation, where young women from other places, even from as far as Mauritania (delivered from captivity thanks to the bishop's financial facilities), come forward for consecration, whereas not one Milanese girl had been "allowed to choose God" by her parents (no. 58).

The conclusion of the "eulogy" composed by Ambrose in honor of ecclesiastical virginity (nos. 62–65), focuses on a very practical issue. In principle, a consecrated virgin should engage herself into the service of the church without caring about her dowry. But in clear and measured terms Ambrose encourages the candidates to ecclesiastical virginity not to neglect the acquisition of their dowry. He does not suggest that it should serve as a donation to the local church or to any kind of canonical institution. He considers it only as a warranty and a social right, securing the open recognition of the spiritual freedom given by Christ to women freed from the legal power of their parents: "Young woman, first conquer filial affection. First you conquer your home, then you conquer the world" (no. 63). The apology ends on the pleasant note of a devotional story (no. 64).

No further doctrinal arguments were broached. Ambrose had said all that he wanted to say, in particular to the parents who dominated the choices of their daughters in his community. A further analysis would certainly highlight the biblical background of *Concerning Virgins*. It would be a rewarding task to compare Ambrose's beautiful image of the bees, developed from no. 40 to no. 45, with similar images in his famous hymn *Exultet* of the liturgy for the Easter vigil. Certainly there are significant parallels to this apology in other of Ambrose's writings. He was convinced that the very existence of the church legitimated new forms of emancipation inside the rigid structures of the patriarchal family, exactly as he claimed more than once the right of the church to exercise its proper spiritual judgment over the highest authority of the state.

## AUGUSTINE OF HIPPO

### On the First Epistle of John, Sermon X

Near Carthage in Roman North Africa the sixty-one-year-old Augustine, bishop of Hippo, delivered his tenth and last homily on the First Epistle of John, in A.D. 415. At Easter of that year he had interrupted his commentary on the Fourth Gospel, a series totaling as many as 124 sermons. As was his custom, he chose a special topic for the octave of Easter, this time the First Epistle of John. He preached sermons I–VI during the octave and then, having resumed his ordinary themes after the Sunday following Easter, he managed to locate the sermons VII and VIII on 1 John the next weekend, and to preach sermons IX and X on the weekend in the octave of the ascension. In other words, the present sermon X was delivered on the Sunday after ascension in the year A.D. 415. Having reached only v. 3 of 1 John he gave up the project, probably realizing that he would never come to an end in commenting on the Epistle. Sermon X remains incomplete.

At that time Augustine was also engaged in the composition of two of his most important works, *On the Trinity* and *On the City of God*. He completed the first in A.D. 419. The section that would most closely parallel our sermon X on 1 John is books VIII and IX. One finds in them a typically Augustinian synthesis of a philosophy and a theology of love, and it would be most appropriate to read them in the light of the present sermon. With regard to *On the City of God* the only certainty we have is that books I–XI date from A.D. 412–416. In the three years before preaching our sermon, Augustine had also expressed his first reactions about the teaching of Pelagius. It was not yet the bitter controversy of a later period, but it is noticeable that in the same year, A.D. 415, the vigilant bishop of Hippo wrote the anti–Pelagian treatises *On Nature and Grace* and *On the Perfection of Human Justice*.

The tenth homily on 1 John does not express any immediate concern about the doctrinal issues at stake in the dispute with Pelagius. But it focuses directly on the Donatist schism, against which Augustine had been fighting since his first day in the episcopal office. In A.D. 405, ten years earlier, the emperor Honorius had issued severe measures against the Donatists. Our sermon alludes to them at the start of no. 10. In A.D. 410 those measures had been reinforced fruitlessly, and so in organizing a public conference in Carthage in A.D. 411 the Catholic bishops of North Africa had aimed at a political solution inside the churches. Augustine's intervention was decisive at that conference, and many Donatists reconciled themselves with the Catholic church. But in A.D. 415 the situation was still troublesome and confusing. Sermon X on 1 John, like the preceding nine, illustrates the spiritual motivation of the bishop in this dramatic struggle within the African churches.

First of all, Augustine was perfectly aware that a particular church, limiting itself to the territories of the northern provinces of Africa, was condemned to become a sect, and that it could by no means claim to represent the universal, or catholic, body of the faithful. Thus, his sermon protests against the provincial narrow-mindedness of the schismatics. Preaching directly out of the Scripture, Augustine projects a vision of the church characterized by its universality. He addresses his congregation in the pure line of the personal mysticism which he had so brilliantly poured into his *Confessions*, completed about fifteen years earlier. A trinitarian confession of faith is formulated at the closing of no. 2 and in the middle of no. 5. More central is the figure of Christ, according to 1 John 5:1, quoted at the beginning of no. 1: "Whoever believes that Jesus is the Christ . . . " Augustine refers to this quotation in starting nos. 2, 3, and 8. In fact, he never stops speaking of Christ when he preaches his understanding of true Christian love, the main theme of the sermon.

Love is the "work of faith" (no. 1); for the faithful, it is the characteristic stance toward life. Inspired by such a theme, the bishop needed no other incentive for launching his lyrical exhortation. Life is pictured as a running, a hastening through all kinds of experience, in order to reach our own fulfillment. The Christian life has Christ himself as its way and its goal. A dynamic anthropology is sketched by Augustine, thanks to the metaphor of the runner. The crucial choice of the right direction is commented on in no. 1, with the help of Pauline phrases and of allusions to the parable of the prodigal son, together with the Augustinian notion of the "area of dissemblance," where people are liable to lose their authentic selves. In no. 2, this good choice in life is identified as love. Faith means nothing but love: "Without love, faith is in vain." The experience of Christian faith means an inner journey, a constant hastening towards the ultimate Jerusalem. The church itself is on pilgrimage in all its members. The homeland of the faithful is beyond the earthly realities, in heaven, in the infinite transcendence of God. Only love, the absolute love given by God, is able to sustain such an endeavor. The ethical demands of this burning love are evoked in nos. 4 and 5. They call the faithful to overcome any limited goals they might have fixed for their existential purposes, and to love each other in the universality of the body of Christ, which they constitute on earth: "Whatever else you come to, keep going until you arrive at the end . . . in your own country" (no. 5). The same recommendations would be repeated, closer to our times, by John Bunyan, in *The Pilgrim's Progress*. But the differences are obvious. Whereas to his fellow countrymen of the seventeenth century, the pietistic nonconformist inculcated ethical fervor and religious endurance in the narrative frame of a picturesque journey up to the gate of the heavenly city, the African leader of the fifth century considered the metaphors of the way, of the running, and of the rest as biblical symbols revealing the mystery of Christ, the mystical body of the church, the ultimate achievement of the divine economy of salvation. The images themselves teach the essential Christian dogma in Augustine. Augustine elaborates upon other illustrations, lesser in importance than the biblical images, yet significant in their own way: "I have finished the bread by consuming it; I have finished the coat by sewing it" (no. 5); "It is just as if someone wished to kiss you on the head and to trample on your feet" (no. 8); "Consider a person languishing in bed . . . " (no. 9). This preacher is a fine craftsman. He links the daily banality, familiar to his listeners, with the sublime vision which enchants him, the vision of a humanity reconciled with God, its savior. Salvation is no longer presented here in the Athanasian form of a narrative message actualizing the gospel stories in the community of the church. Faith is no longer envisaged as the supernatural recognition of Christ's actual acting in the church, as Athanasius never tired of insisting. In Augustine, the letter of the biblical narratives does not so much become "spiritual" in being "actualized" in the church; rather, it is in the service of a spiritualistic language which comes from elsewhere, from a more philosophical longing for divine transcendency. Thus, Augustine preaches on the unity of the universal church, in stressing the character of its fundamental quest in the light of his own theological notion of love which was permeated with the purest ideals of his Christianized variant of Neoplatonism. This is the thought that overflowed in these outbursts of mystical enthusiasm: as we read in sermon X, "The rule of charity, my brothers, its vigor, its flowers, fruit, beauty, charm, its food, drink, nourishment, and its embrace is without satiety" (no. 7).

## ROMANOS THE MELODIST

### *Through the Coming of Your Holy Spirit*

Romanos the Singer, the "Melodist" in Greek, was born around A.D. 490 in Emesa, Syria. He became a deacon of the Anastasis church in Constantinople, where Gregory of Nazianzus had already reached the peak of celebrity as a preacher over a century before. No fewer than a thousand hymns, in Greek *kontakia*, constitute his literary legacy. Assumed within the Byzantine liturgy, these kontakia usually contained over twenty strophes, with a meter no longer determined by the quantity of the syllables, as was still the rule in more refined court poetry, but only by the normal stressing of the words in the spoken Greek.

Romanos seems to have enjoyed an immediate popularity. His hymns for Christmas and for Easter offer a blend of substantial theological motifs interwoven with charming references to popular devotion. The richness of his imagination never led him astray from his pastoral purposes. He is a singing preacher and a true poet, fusing together the Greek repertoire of early Christian songs with the pious sensitivity of his Syriac background. From the tenth century on, the songs of Romanos never failed to be acclaimed in the Byzantine church as classics among liturgical hymnody.

This hymn *Through the Coming of Your Holy Spirit* has been composed for the Vespers of Pentecost. By stark contrast, the penitential prostration of the faithful underlines the vigorous lifting up of their theological awareness. Each strophe abounds in implicit references to Scripture and to the traditional Christian doctrine of salvation. The Nicene notion of the Trinity, from strophe 1 on, provides the foundation for the elaboration of more lyrical themes treating the salvific acting of the Spirit. In strophe 3, the newness of the Christian revelation and in strophe 4, the final destruction of idolatry, are both recalled in the style of past apologetics. The litany of the metaphorical titles given to the

Spirit in strophe 5 combines symbols taken over from the Gospels and from Revelation. In strophe 6 the hymn culminates in a Trinitarian doxology.

## MAXIMUS THE CONFESSOR

### *Introduction to Question 48*

This selection of early sources concludes with a mere token selection from Maximus. Such a voice is appropriate at the completion of this series of spiritual witnesses, as Maximus epitomized in his personal experience the most distinctive mystical achievements of the five centuries of Christian spirituality. It was as a martyr that he died on 13 August, 662, at the age of 80 in Lazika, on the eastern shore of the Black Sea; among other ill treatments, his tongue was torn out and his right hand cut off by the police of the Byzantine emperor. He was a theological genius, perhaps even greater than Origen, Gregory of Nyssa, and Augustine together, and recapitulated in a christological synthesis all the dogmatic traditions developed in the Greek-speaking churches during the first half-millennium of Christianity. He was a monk, after having served in a high rank in the imperial court. This frail monk became the fearless defender of doctrinal freedom in matters of faith against the all-powerful administration of the Byzantine emperor. At the time of the spectacular conquest of Syria and Egypt by an expansionist Islam (A.D. 636–657), religious politics in Byzantium were considered only a means for holding together, if possible, the remaining parts of the vanishing Roman Empire in the Orient. Maximus opposed such politics, which included a betrayal of the christological dogma defined at Chalcedon in A.D. 451.

His theological work, immense in regard to the broad culture it implies, was of a degree of penetration unique in the whole of patristic literature. Even the technicalities of his learned language are without parallel among the church fathers. Much work has been done in our times, and much more needs to be pursued, in order to investigate the riches of Maximus's doctrines.

His prayer to the incarnate Logos offers a remarkable epilogue to the present collection. The concentration of his style is characterized by biblical images and allusions, but more than anything else it expresses the silent joy and the luminous certitude of a faith well assumed by the mind of a great mystic.

# II.

### ODE 37

I extended my hands towards the Lord
and toward the Most High I lifted up my voice.

I spoke with the lips of my heart
and he heard as my cry rose before him.

His Word came toward me
and gave me the fruits of my labor
—gave me rest through the grace of the Lord.

Hallelujah.

## ODE 40

As honey flows from the comb of the bee,
As milk from a mother's tender nursing
So my hope is upon you, my God.

As a fountain gushes forth its waters
So my heart overflows in praise of the Lord
And my lips cry aloud his greatness.

My tongue is sweetened by his anthems
My members anointed by his odes,
My face uplifted in his exultations
My spirit rejoicing in his love,
My inmost self radiant in him.

Those in awe of him will yet trust in him,
Salvation will be assured in him.

Life undying is his possession
Incorruptible are those who receive of it.

Hallelujah.

# III.

## The Martyrs of Lyon

The servants of Christ of Vienne and Lyon in Gaul greet those of the family of faith in Asia and Phrygia who hold the same faith and hope of redemption—peace and grace and glory from God the Father and from Jesus Christ our Lord.

There can be no adequate description, either in word or writing of the magnitude of the suffering here, of the animosity of the pagans towards the saints, or of the steadfastness of the blessed martyrs.

The adversary hurtled down in full force—a prelude indeed to his final coming of which we can be sure. He left nothing undone to train and prepare his forces against the servants of God. Consequently, we were not only shut out of houses, out of the baths and the public square, but also forbidden to appear in any public place whatsoever.

Taking the field against him was the grace of God, protecting the weak, on the one hand, and on the other, setting up sturdy pillars (cf. Rev. 3:12; 1 Tim. 3:15) who, through their qualities of endurance, were able to draw upon themselves all the attacks of the evil one. As the battle closed about them, these endured all manner of insult and punishment, deeming these sufferings insignificant as they hastened towards Christ, thus demonstrating "the suffering of the present to be as nothing compared with the glory to be revealed in us" (Rom. 8:18).

First of all, they endured with dignity and courage the screams of insult, the buffeting, the dragging this way and that. They were hemmed in, despoiled, stoned—in short they endured everything that an enraged mob tends to inflict upon the objects of their hatred. Then, dragged into the public square by the tribune and the city magistrates, they were questioned before the whole populace. On publicly confessing their faith, they were locked up in prison to await the arrival of the governor.

Then, when they had been led before the governor, who indulged in the usual kind of cruelty meted out to us, one of our brothers, Vettius Epagathus, stepped forward—a man filled with the love of God and his neighbor. Though still young, his manner of life had reached such an estimable level that to him could be justly applied what had been said of the saintly old Zachariah— that he had followed blamelessly all the commandments and ordinances of the Lord (Luke 1:6), that he was unwearied in the service of his neighbor and that he was possessed of great zeal for God and fervor of spirit. His character being such, he could not endure the unreasonableness of the judgment passed on us, and in his indignation asked that he might speak on our behalf to dispute the charge of atheism and irreligious conduct.

In spite of his distinguished bearing, those around the tribunal shouted him down, and the governor disallowed his just plea, and instead put to him the single question "Are you a Christian?" Answering in the clearest tones, the young man confessed his faith, and thus threw in his lot with the martyr band. Styled the advocate of the Christians, he had indeed the Advocate (cf. John 14:16; Luke 1:67) within, the Spirit that filled Zachariah. And to this he attested by the plenitude of his love. He was only too glad to lay down his life for his fellow Christians (cf. 1 John 3:16), for he was and is a true disciple of Christ, "following the Lamb wherever he goes" (Rev. 14:4).

From this point, the rest could be divided into two groups— those clearly ready to be the first martyrs, who fully confessed their faith in unbounded enthusiasm. But it was apparent that others were still untrained, ill prepared, and weak, and quite unable to bear the strain of the great conflict—of this number, ten were stillborn. This defection caused us immeasurable grief and pain; indeed it was a circumstance that blunted the enthusiasm among the remainder who had not yet been arrested. Yet, in spite of the threat of dire sufferings, these continued to attend the martyrs and would not desert them.

It was at this stage that we suffered deeply with regard to the uncertainty of the confession of faith—not because of the torments that we might have to endure, but because, in the final reckoning, some of our number might fall away. However, day by day, those of the community held in highest esteem were arrested to fill up the numbers, with the result that from the two churches those most outstanding for their zeal and their qualities of leadership were assembled together.

At the same time, certain pagans among our household servants were arrested, for the governor had ordered a full investigation into our activities. These servants, caught in the snares of Satan, were terrified by the tortures inflicted on the blessed ones, and, following the promptings of the soldiers, they gave false evidence as to our involvement in all kinds of evil practices—murderous Thyestean banquets, Oedipodean practices, and so on, things difficult even to contemplate in human behavior. As these accusations were noised abroad, everyone was incensed at us. Even those who previously through friendship had inclined to moderation, now were consumed with anger. Thus was fulfilled the Lord's saying, "the time is coming when anyone who put you to death will claim to be serving God" (John 16:2). After that, the suffering of the holy martyrs defies description, as from that point Satan's most urgent endeavor was to wring out some confirmation of these blasphemies.

All the fury of the crowd, the governor and the soldiers alike was now concentrated upon Sanctus, the deacon from Vienne, and Maturus, though newly baptized, a noble athlete in the faith, and upon Attalus of Pergamum, indeed a "pillar and ground" (1 Tim. 3:15), of the community there, and also upon Blandina. It was through this woman that Christ demonstrated that what is regarded as insignificant, unsightly, and even contemptible in the common opinion is to be accounted honorable in the sight of God, as she demonstrated her love for God in dynamic action, not in empty boasting.

We were all in a state of terror—her earthly mistress, too, who was herself one of the martyrs in the conflict—lest, Blandina, by reason of her physical frailty, would not be able to make a bold confession of faith. But she was filled with such power, that even those taking turns to torture her in every possible way from morning till night had to admit defeat. They could do nothing further, and wondered that she still breathed when her whole body was a mass of open wounds. They swore that any one of these tortures was sufficient of itself to cause death—let alone so many and of such a nature. Yet this blessed woman was renewed in her vigor through her confession of faith. Indeed the very saying of the words "I am a Christian—we have done nothing to be ashamed of" was itself a restoration, a means of refreshment effecting an insensibility to suffering.

As for Sanctus, he too endured with extraordinary, indeed with superhuman courage, all that inhumanity could devise. These evil men were hoping that through the persistence and the severity of the application of their tortures, he would be forced into some admission; but he would not even divulge his own name, or his nationality or city, or whether he was a slave or freedman. To all their questions he replied in Latin, "I am a Christian." This he confessed over and over. In place of his name, city, or nationality, or any other thing, the crowd heard not another sound from his lips.

All this but deepened the determination of the governor and his torturers to beat him, and so as a last resort they applied red-hot metal to the most sensitive parts of his body. But this measure, in spite of the actual scalding, found Sanctus himself utterly resolute in his confession of faith, his spirit cooled and strengthened by the heavenly fountain whose life-giving waters flow from the side of Christ (cf. John 4:10; 7:38; 19:34; Rev. 21:6). However, his body gave ample witness to the reality of his sufferings—the whole an open wound, battered, twisted beyond human recognition. But it was in this form that Christ suffered and achieved great glory—vanquishing the adversary and giving an example to all the others that there is nothing to be feared where there is the Father's love (1 John 4:18), and nothing painful where there is the glory of Christ (2 Cor. 8:23).

A few days later, the wicked men again tortured the martyr. They thought that the swelling and the inflammation of his body was such that another application of the same tortures would overcome him—especially at a time when he could not bear the slightest touch. On the other hand, if he died under torture, this would instill fear in the rest of the group. Not only did those expectations come to nothing, but to their utter amazement, his poor body straightened out and regained its former shape and the use of the limbs. In fact, through the grace of Christ, the second round of tortures proved to be a healing, rather than a further battering.

One of those who had apostatized was a woman named Biblis. The devil, considering her already well in his grip, thought he would gain further ground through her blasphemies. He held her as one cowardly and easily intimidated out of the tortures in the hope of dragging out of her some impious accusations against us. But once she was bound to the rack, she came to her senses, as if coming out of a deep sleep. The prospect of these temporal punishments awakened a vivid awareness of the eternal vengeance in Gehenna (Matt. 5:22; Mark 9:45). Thus she even contradicted the blasphemies, saying, "How could such people eat children when they are not even allowed to consume the blood of irrational animals?" From that point, she confessed herself to be a Christian, and was listed among those who had thrown in their lot with the martyrs.

Since these tyrannous plans had been completely overcome by Christ through the constancy of the blessed ones, the devil began to devise other  methods of torture such as cramped and dark imprisonment, and racking to the fifth notch—these and every other outrage which those inspired by the devil are accustomed to inflict upon their prisoners. In consequence, the greater number of the martyrs were suffocated in prison—but just as many as the Lord intended to pass out of life in this manner, thus showing forth his glory.

Others were tortured so severely that it seemed they could not survive even if they received every medical attention, yet they continued to survive in their imprisonment. Deprived of every vestige of human care, they were strengthened by the Lord, and so empowered in soul and body, they continued to urge and to exhort the others. But the young and those recently arrested who were physically ill prepared to face the extremes of imprisonment perished in that place.

The blessed Pothinus, too, who was entrusted with the ministry of the episcopacy of Lyon, was dragged before the tribunal. Though more than ninety years of age and physically frail, his breathing difficult because of his many infirmities, yet through his intense desire for martyrdom, he found the strength which stems from a zealous spirit. Though his body was wasted by age and disease, yet he held on to the soul within him that Christ might walk in triumph in it (cf. 2 Cor. 2:14). Conducted to the tribunal by the soldiers, while the civil authorities and the whole crowd full of clamor surged along with him (cf. Luke 23:18–23)—as if he were Christ himself—Pothinus indeed gave noble witness.

When questioned by the governor as to who was the God of the Christians he replied, "If you are found worthy you will know."

At this, he was dragged around mercilessly and beaten from all sides. Those nearby attacked him with hands and feet in complete disregard for his age, while those farther off threw whatever came to hand. Everyone acted as if it were a great shame or even a sacrilege to abstain from any form of indignity that they could heap upon him. They believed that this was the way to avenge their own gods. Scarcely breathing, he was thrown into prison and died there two days later.

It was at this point that an extraordinary providence became manifest, and the boundless mercy of Jesus was revealed to an extent rarely experienced in the communities of faith, but certainly not beyond the art of Christ. For on the one hand those who in the process of the first arrest had denied the faith, and yet had been imprisoned with the rest and shared the horrors of confinement, found that their denial was of no advantage at all. On the other hand, the ones who confessed themselves to be Christians, were held on that charge alone, whereas the former group were charged with murder and all manner of foul crimes and were punished twice as much as their companions.

What is more, the joy of martyrdom, the hope of what had been promised them—in their love for Christ and through the Spirit of the Father—all this lightened their burden of suffering for the confessors. But the deniers, deeply troubled in conscience as they were, were all easily distinguishable from the others as they came through the passageway. The confessors came forward, their faces aglow with nobility and grace so that they wore the chains clasped to them like lovely ornaments, like the bride adorned in embroidered apparel of gold (cf. Ps. 45:12–15). At the same time they exuded the fragrance of Christ (2 Cor. 2:15), so that it seemed that they had anointed themselves with a perfume of this world.

The contrast was sharp. The others were gloomy, dejected, and filled with shame, and to add to their misery, they were reviled by the crowd as mean-spirited and cowardly. They found themselves called murderers, having given up the most honorable, esteemed, and life-giving Name of all.

When the rest of the community saw this, they were confirmed in their resolution, and those who were arrested confessed their faith without hesitation, and without giving ear to the sophistry of the devil.

In the days that followed, the witness they gave in their exodus from this life took many different forms. And out of a great variety of flowers and colors they wove a single crown and offered it to the Father. It is indeed fitting that, after enduring a contest of so many forms and culminating in a great victory, these noble athletes received the glorious crown of incorruption (cf. 1 Cor. 9:25; 15:42, 50, 53).

And so it was that Maturus, Sanctus, Blandina, and Attalus were led into the amphitheater to be exposed to the beast as a public spectacle of the inhumanity of the crowd, for the day given over to the animal contests had been carefully arranged on our account.

Maturus and Sanctus went through the whole torturous course in the amphitheater just as if they had suffered nothing beforehand—or rather, as if having triumphed in the earlier contests, now they faced the final conflict for the crown itself. Once again, according to local custom they endured the gauntlet of whips, the mauling of the animals, and anything else the maddened crowd screamed and urged from all sides. To crown all this, they were seated in the iron chair, on which their bodies were scorched so that they were enveloped with the smoke of burning flesh. But even this did not suffice, and the mob increased their demands, wishing to overcome the martyrs' constancy. As for Sanctus, they heard nothing other than which he had repeated over and over from the outset—his confession of faith.

Through all the mighty contest they had remained steadfast in soul and now were finally sacrificed. All day long, in place of the many forms of gladiatorial combat these had indeed become a spectacle to the world. All the while Blandina, hanging from a stake, was exposed as bait for the wild beasts which had been loosed for the attack. She seemed to hang there in the form of a cross and continued to inspire with great enthusiasm those still struggling in the combat. In the midst of their anguish, through their sister it seemed to them that they saw with the eyes of their bodies, him who was crucified for them so that he might convince those who believed in him that all who suffer for Christ's glory will have eternal fellowship with the living God.

But since none of the beasts had touched her, Blandina was taken down from the stake and led back to prison to be under strict guard before facing the next trial. So, being victorious in even further contests, she would make the condemnation of the "crooked serpent" (Isa. 27:1) even more inescapable. This woman, little, weak, easily despised, had put on (Rom. 13:14) the mighty and invincible warrior, Christ, and throughout the many rounds allotted to her in the combat had forcibly overthrown the adversary, and through her contest had won the crown of incorruption (cf. 1 Cor. 9:25; 1 Pet. 5:4).

Attalus, too, was loudly demanded by the crowd, for he was of high renown; he came forward a ready combatant. This was by reason of his clear conscience, seeing that he had been well and truly trained in the Christian discipline and had always been a witness among us to the truth. He was led right around the amphitheater behind a sign on which was written in Latin "This is Attalus, the Christian," while the mob erupted in violent anger against him. However, when the governor learned that he was a Roman citizen, he ordered that he be locked up with others who were in prison. It was in reference to these Roman citizens that he had sent to the emperor and was waiting the imperial decision.

The intervening period was neither idle nor fruitless (cf. 2 Pet. 1:8) for them, but through their constancy, the boundless mercy of Christ was revealed. For through the living, the dead were being brought back to life. The martyrs continued to mediate grace to those who had failed in their witness, and the virgin mother found great joy in receiving back alive those who had been stillborn. For through the martyrs, the greater number of those who had denied the faith were redirected onto the path of life. Conceived again and quickened in the womb, they learned to confess the faith. Alive now and braced for action, they approached the tribunal to be questioned again by the governor. (For God who does not desire the death of the sinner, but rather gives the grace of repentance, was making it sweet for them [cf. 1 Tim. 2:4].)

The emperor's instructions were that the confessors were to be executed, but that those who denied were to be released. The festival which attracted great crowds of people from all the various regions was about to start, and it was to this that the governor had the blessed martyrs brought up before the tribunal to use them as a spectacle and a processional for the crowds. With this in mind, he interrogated them once more, and as many as were believed to be Roman citizens he beheaded. The rest he condemned to the beasts.

So it was that Christ was greatly glorified in those who had denied the faith at the former occasion, but who now, contrary to the expectation of the pagans, made public confession. They had been examined in a group apart from the rest, in consideration of the certainty of their release, but upon their confession of faith they were added to the numbers of the martyrs. Outside of such ranks there remained those who lacked even a trace of faith, who never had any experience of the wedding garment (Matt. 22:11) nor even a notion of the fear of God, but who in their very manner of life blasphemed the Way. These were the very sons of perdition (John 17:12). But all the rest were added to the church.

Close to those being examined was a certain Alexander, a Phrygian by birth and a physician by profession. He had spent many years in different regions of Gaul and was known by almost everyone because of his love for God and his openness in preaching the Word, for certainly he was not lacking in a share of the apostolic charism. He had been standing in front of the tribunal and encouraged the Christians in their confession of faith (by his gestures of support). It was apparent to those standing around the tribunal that he was as one giving birth. The crowd, thoroughly enraged that those who had denied on a former occasion now confessed the faith anew, cried out against Alexander as the one responsible for the change. The governor ordered him to appear before him and give an account of himself. When Alexander affirmed that he was a Christian, the enraged governor condemned him to the beasts.

Thus, on the following day Alexander entered the arena in the company of Attalus—for the governor, wishing to gratify the crowd, consigned Attalus to the beasts once more. Those men went through all of the instruments of tortures devised for the amphitheater and having steadfastly endured the most intense conflict were sacrificed in the end. All the while Alexander had neither groaned nor uttered the slightest complaint but communed with God within his heart.

Attalus, on the other hand, as he was fastened to the bronze chair addressed the crowd in Latin, "Look, what you are doing is cannibalism! We are not cannibals, nor do we practice any other kind of vileness." Being asked what was the name of God, he replied, "God does not have a name as a human being does."

On the final day of the single combats, Blandina was brought back again together with Ponticus, a boy of fifteen. Every day they had been brought in to watch the rest being tortured, and these had been attempts to force them to take the oath by the pagan idols. Through steadfast perseverance they had rejected such attempts with contempt so that the crowd became angered against them, reserving neither pity for the age of the boy nor respect for the woman. On the contrary, they were exposed to every horror and dragged through the whole cycle of tortures in an effort to force them to take the oath, but without the least success.

Urged on by his sister in Christ (to the pagans it was obvious that she was encouraging and strengthening him), Ponticus, having nobly endured all the tortures, gave up his spirit. As for the blessed Blandina, last of all, like a noble mother (2 Macc. 7:20–23) having encouraged her children and sent them on before her in triumph to the King, she herself set out on the path of her children's suffering, hastening towards them, rejoicing and exulting because of her own exodus as one being invited to a bridal feast (Rev. 19:9) rather than as one being thrown to the beasts.

After the scourging, after the wild animals, after the red-hot grid, finally she was cast into a net and exposed to a bull. She was severely tossed by the animal yet was hardly aware of what was happening because of her hope and her grasp of all that she believed in and her communion with Christ. At last she was sacrificed, but the pagans themselves confessed that never had any woman suffered so much and so intensely.

But not even this was enough to satisfy the madness of their savagery towards the saints, because a wild and barbarous people once inflamed by a wild beast are not easily held in check, and their viciousness took on a further particularity in regard to their treatment of the corpses.

They experienced no shame in their defeat since they lacked the human ability to reason; on the contrary, in them, as in a wild beast, this defeat inflamed their anger. Thus the governor and the crowd showed us the same unmerited anger in fulfillment of the Scriptures. "Let the wicked be wicked and the righteous perform righteousness" (cf. Rev. 22:11; Dan. 12:10). They threw the bodies of those who had died of suffocation in prison to the dogs and kept the most careful guard by night and day lest any be buried by us. And whatever remained of those who had been exposed to the beasts, or to the fire, or burnt and torn apart, heads and severed sections of bodies—all were left unburied under military guard for days on end.

Even then, there were those who continued to rave and gnash their teeth as if they sought some further extremity by way of vengeance against the martyrs. Others laughed and jeered, at the same time magnifying their own idols and ascribing to them the punishment of the Christians. Others again, though more sympathetic, frequently reproached us, "Where is your God?" (Ps. 42:4). What profit was there in their religious convictions which they preferred even to their very lives?

These were the different attitudes they expressed. But as for us, we were plunged into grief because we were not able to bury the bodies in the earth. Darkness did not come to our aid; nor did money persuade or earnest entreaty cause them any shame. But in every possible way, they maintained the strictest guard as if it were of some great benefit for them to prevent the burial.

After the bodies of the martyrs had been subjected to every possible insult and had lain exposed to the elements for six days, these wicked people burned the remains and swept the ashes into the Rhone which flows close by. They were determined that not a trace be left on the face of the earth.

The pagans acted as if they had won a victory over God and had deprived the martyrs of their regeneration. With this intention they kept saying that the martyrs "might have no hope of the resurrection, in which they had put their trust when they introduced this strange new cult among us. And with no fear of the tortures they went forward readily and joyfully to death. Now let us see if they will rise again and whether God can come to their aid, and deliver them out of our hands?" (cf. Wisd. of Sol. 2:17–18; Dan. 3:15; 6:20).

(To conclude the account, Eusebius selects a number of passages from the document which treat the concept of martyrdom itself and further describe the spirit of kindness and generosity which animated the martyrs.)

The martyrs were very eager to imitate Christ, "who being in the form of God did not deem equality with God something to be grasped at" (Phil. 2:6). Though they had won such glory, and not just once or twice but many times had given witness, though brought from the combats with the beasts covered with wounds and scarred from the branding, yet still they would not call themselves martyrs. Nor would they allow any of us by word or by letter to refer to them with such a title and sharply rebuked such attempts.

Gladly they allowed the name "martyr" as a title to Christ alone—the faithful and true witness, the firstborn from the dead and the prince of the life of God (cf. Rev. 1:5; 3:14). Then they would recall the martyrs who had already passed away and would say, "These were indeed martyrs. Christ deemed them worthy to accept their confession of faith, placing his seal on their witness by their death. On the other hand, we are only ordinary confessors." Then tearfully they would appeal to their fellow Christians for earnest prayers so that their confession would be brought to its perfection. Though they plainly demonstrated the power of martyrdom by their works and by their openness when they appeared before the pagans, and though they gave ample evidence of their nobility through steadfastness and intrepid conduct, yet, still filled with the fear of God, they continued to refuse the title, of martyr.

They humbled themselves under that mighty hand by which now they have been exalted (cf. 1 Peter 5:6). They defended the faith to all, but they accused no one; they loosed all, but they bound none. They prayed for those who had treated them so cruelly, as did the perfect martyr Stephen: "Lord, do not blame them for this sin" (Acts 7:60). If he prayed for those who were stoning him, how much more on behalf of his fellow Christians?

Because of the sincerity of their love, this became the greatest of the battles against the Adversary. The Beast had to be throttled to be forced to disgorge alive those who had been devoured. They did not boast over the ones who had fallen. On the contrary, of their riches they gave to those in need and with motherly tenderness went and pleaded with the Father on their behalf. They asked for life, and he gave it to them, and they shared it with their neighbor when they went forth to God in complete triumph. Having always loved peace and always commended peace, in peace they departed to God. They left no distress for their Mother nor division or conflict in the family of the faith, but rather joy, peace, harmony, and love.

# IV.

## Clement of eAlexandria

### EXHORTATION TO THE GREEKS

I could cite ten thousand passages from Scripture for you, not "the smallest detail of which will pass away" (Matt. 5:18; Luke 16:17) without being fulfilled, for the mouth of the Lord—the Holy Spirit—has said it. "My child, no longer ignore the instructions of the Lord, nor be discouraged by his reproaches" (Prov. 3:11). What an overwhelming love for humankind! It is not as a teacher to his pupils, nor as a master to his servants, nor as a god to human beings, but as a tender father (*Odyssey* 2.47) that he admonishes his children. Moses confesses that he is "in fear and trembling" (Heb. 12:21) upon hearing the word, but you, listening to the very Word of God, are you not fearful? Are you not deeply concerned? Are you not at the same time being extremely cautious, and yet at the same time very eager for instruction—that is eager for salvation—as you fear the anger, love the grace, and strive after hope in order to avoid the judgment?

Come, come, my young people! Young because "unless you are born again" (John 3:3) and because "as little children" (Matt. 18:3), as the Scripture says, you will not recover the One who is indeed Father, nor "will you ever enter the kingdom of heaven" (John 3:5). How is it possible for a stranger to inherit? It is, I think, whenever such a one is registered and given citizenship, and receives formal adoption, then will he be concerned with what belongs to the Father (Luke 2:49), then will he be counted worthy to possess the inheritance, then will he share the kingdom of the Father, with the Begotten One, the Dearly Beloved (Matt. 3:17; Mark 1:11; Luke 3:22; John 1:34). For this is the assembly of the firstborn, which is composed of many good children. These are "the firstborn who have been inscribed in the heavens" and who celebrate their festivals with "ten thousand angels" (Heb. 12:22). We are these firstborn children, we, those nourished by God the true friends of the "First Born" (Rom. 8:29; Col. 1:15), the first of all the human family to have known God, the first to have been cut off from sin, the first to have been torn away from the devil.

But now, the more God turns in love toward the human race, the more do some turn from the divine. For while God wishes to take us out of slavery to become his children, these disdain to become his children. What gross stupidity! You stand shamed before the Lord! He promises freedom, you take flight into slavery! He grants salvation, you plunge back into mortal coils! He offers eternal life, you hold out for punishment and prefer "the fire which the Lord has prepared for the devil and his angels" (Matt. 25:41). This is why the blessed apostle wrote, "I give witness in the Lord that you must no longer live as the pagans do— their minds empty, their understanding darkened. They are estranged from the life of God because of their ignorance and their resistance; without remorse they have abandoned themselves to lust and to the indulgence of every sort of immorality" (Eph. 4:17–19). When such a witness reproves human folly and calls upon the Lord to hear, what else remains to the unbelieving but judgment and condemnation. But the Lord does not grow weary of admonishing, of frightening, of exhorting, arousing, and warning. He rouses those who have been sleeping; and those who have been wandering, he raises out of the darkness itself. "Awake," he says, "you who are asleep; arise from the dead, and upon you will shine Christ" (Eph. 5:14) the Lord—he who is the sun of the Resurrection, he who is begotten before the Day Star (Ps. 109:3, LXX), he who bestows life through his own radiance.

Let no one, then, despise the Word, lest unwittingly he despises himself. For the Scripture says somewhere, "Today, if you hear his voice, do not harden your hearts, as in the provocation in the desert, when your fathers put me to the test" (Heb. 3:7–11; Ps. 95:8–11). Do you wish to learn what this "test" is? The Holy Spirit goes on to explain it to you. "And they saw my works," he says, "for forty years; therefore I was angered against this generation and said, always they wander in their heart, but they did not know my ways as I swore in my anger, they shall not enter into my rest."

See the threat! See the exhortation! See the penalty! How is it that we still exchange grace for wrath and do not open our ears to the Word and welcome God into souls that are unstained. Great is the grace of his promise if "today we hear his voice." The "today" is extended to each and every day, as long as a "today" is named. Both the "today" and the teaching continue until the consummation of time; and then the true "today" which is the unending day of God extends throughout the endless ages. Then let us always obey the voice of the divine Word, for "today" is an image of eternity, while the day is a symbol of the light, and the light of humankind is the Word through whom we look upon God.

It is only to be expected then that grace will superabound for those who have believed and have obeyed; while those who have been unbelieving, and wandering in their hearts, not knowing the Lord's paths, which John commanded to make straight and to prepare—with such as these God is angered and threatening. And indeed figuratively the ancient Hebrews in their wanderings received the fulfillment of the threat; for, because of their unbelief they were not to "enter into the Rest" (Ps. 95:11) until, having closely followed the successor of Moses, at last they learned by their own experience that they could not be saved other than believing as Jesus (Joshua) did.

But the Lord, being the lover of all humankind, encourages all to the exact knowledge of the truth (1 Tim. 2:4), and sends the Paraclete. What is the "exact knowledge"?—godliness; and according to Paul, "Godliness is profitable for all things, having promise of the life which now is, and of that which is to come" (1 Tim. 4:8). If eternal salvation were offered for sale, how much, O my people, would you agree to lay out over and above? Not even if one were to give the whole Pactolus, the legendary river of gold, could one pay the price equivalent to salvation.

But do not be discouraged. You can, if you wish, buy this most precious salvation with treasure of your own, with love and faith, which is a payment worthy of life. This price God accepts with pleasure, "for we have set our hope upon the living God, who is the savior of all, especially those who believe" (1 Tim. 4:10). The rest, clinging to this world, as certain seaweed clings to the rocks of the sea (*Republic* 611D), have little esteem for immortality. Like the old man of Ithaca they yearn for neither truth nor the heavenly homeland, nor for the real and true light, but for smoke of the hearth fire (*Odyssey* 1.57–58). Now when godliness seeks to make a person as like to God as possible, it ascribes as a suitable teacher, God, who worthily has the power to impress upon the human person the likeness to God. Knowing this teaching to be truly divine, the apostle says, "and you, Timothy, from your infancy have known the sacred letters, the source of the wisdom which through faith in Christ leads to salvation" (2 Tim. 3:15). For the letters which make sacred and make divine are sacred in very truth, and out of these sacred letters and syllables are composed the Scriptures, which have been collected together. In consequence, the apostle calls these Scriptures "inspired of God," "useful for teaching, for reproach, for correction, for instruction in righteousness, so that the man of God may be fully prepared and equipped for every good work" (2 Tim. 3:16, 17). No one could be as moved by the exhortations of the other saints as by those of the Lord himself who so loves the human race. For nothing other than this one endeavor is his—to save the human race. Therefore he cries aloud urging them toward salvation, "The Kingdom of heaven is at hand" (Matt. 4:17). Those drawing near through fear, he turns to repentance. In this way the apostle in appealing to the Macedonians becomes an interpreter of the divine voice when he says, "The Lord is at hand (Phil. 4:5); take care lest we be found empty." But you have so little fear, or rather you are lacking in faith so that you neither obey the Lord himself, nor Paul who entreats on behalf of Christ.

"O taste and see that God is good" (cf. Ps. 34:12). Faith will lead you in, experience will teach, the Scripture will instruct, saying, "Come, children, listen to me; I will teach you the fear of the Lord," and then speaking as if to those who have already believed, it adds briefly, "Who wishes for life and desires to see good days?" We shall answer, we who are worshipers of the good and who are zealous for good things. Listen, then "you who are far off," listen "you who are near at hand" (Isa. 57:19; Eph. 2:17), the Word is hidden from no one. Light is shared by all, it shines on all people. In the Word, no one can be a Cimmerian (*Odyssey* 11.13–16—a land of darkness). Let us hasten toward salvation, toward regeneration. Let us, who are many, hasten to be drawn together into one love, according to the unity of the One who is single in essence. In a similar way, let us who are being made holy, pursue unity—we who are seeking the good Monad. The union of many into one, blending into a divine harmony out of separate and dissonant sounds, becomes one symphony; it follows the lead of the single choirmaster and teacher, the Word. It finds its rest in truth itself when it cries, "Abba, Father!" (Rom. 8:15). God welcomes this, the true cry issuing from his children, the first fruit of the harvest.

# V.

## Athanasius of Alexandria

### ON THE INTERPRETATION
### OF THE PSALMS

1. My dear Marcellinus, I admire your resolute conduct in
Christ, for in addition to bearing up well in the present trial with
all the suffering it entails, you do not neglect the practices of the
spiritual life. I made anxious inquiries of the bearer of your letter,
and what do I hear that you have been doing during the course of
your illness? You have devoted this enforced leisure to the study
of the whole of the sacred Scriptures, and most frequently it is to
the Book of Psalms that you have turned with special attention,
all the while being eagerly engaged in the task of trying to grasp
the inner meaning of every single psalm.

This is excellent. I, myself, have a particular fondness for this
book, as indeed, for the whole of the Scriptures. It was because of
this text that I came to possess what I wish to write down for you.
I used to have long discussions with an old man deeply versed in
his studies. Clasping the Psalter to him, he explained it carefully
to me and there is no doubt that he possessed a certain gracious
and persuasive thoughtfulness in his narration. This is what he
said.

2. My child, as it is written, "all of our Scriptures," both old
and new, "are divinely inspired and useful for instruction" (2
Tim. 3:16). But to those who devote themselves to it with special
care, the Book of Psalms merits very close attention. It is true that
every book of the Scriptures enjoys the ministry of its own particular message. The Pentateuch speaks of the beginning of the
world, of the deeds of the Patriarchs, of the exodus of Israel from
Egypt, and of the giving of the Law. The Triteuch (Joshua, Judges,
Ruth) describe the allotment to the tribes of Israel, the acts of the

Judges and the genealogy of David, the books of Kings and Parali-
pomenon (Chronicles) record the deeds of the kings, and the
Book of Esdras (Ezra), the deliverance from the captivity, the
return of the people, and the building of the temple and the city.
The prophets foretell the coming of the Savior, call to mind the
commandments, rebuke sinners, and deliver prophecies to the
Gentiles.

However, the Book of Psalms, like a blessed garden bearing
many different fruits, contains the themes of the other books in
its songs, while at the same time its own particular ministry is
clearly demonstrated alongside of what it sings of the others.

3. It sings the themes of Genesis in Psalm 19, "The heavens
declare the glory of God, and the firmament proclaims the works
of his hands." And in 24, "The Lord's is the earth and its fullness,
the world and all those who dwell in it. He has founded it upon
the seas."

What especially belongs to the books Exodus, Numbers, and
Deuteronomy is well sung in Psalms 78 and 114, "When Israel
came out of Egypt, the house of Jacob from a people of alien
tongue, Judah became his sanctuary, and Israel his domain" and it
sings the following in Psalm 105, "He sent Moses, his servant;
Aaron whom he had chosen. He placed among them the works of
his signs and wonders in the land of Ham. He sent forth the darkness and it grew dark, yet they disobeyed his words. He turned
their waters into blood, and killed their fish. Their land swarmed
with frogs, even in the storehouses of their kings. He spoke, and
there came swarms of flies and gnats throughout their borders."

Actually throughout the whole of this psalm and in 106 the
exodus narrative is to be found in outline.

The priesthood and the tabernacle is proclaimed in Psalm 28
which refers to the going forth of the tabernacle (LXX heading Ps.
28).

"Bring to the Lord, sons of God, bring to the Lord offspring of
rams, bring to the Lord glory and honor."

4. The books of Joshua and Judges are indicated in Psalm 107,
"They built cities to dwell in; they sowed fields and planted
vines." For it was under Joshua, son of Nun, that the promised
land passed into their hands. In the same psalm when it says a
number of times, "and they cried out to the Lord in their oppres-
sion, and he saved them from their distress," the Book of Judges is
indicated because it was then that whenever they cried out to

him, he sent them judges according to the need of the moment, and thus he saved the people from their oppressors.

In Psalm 20 we hear of the themes of the Book of Kings, "some are strong in chariots, some in horses, but we will be strengthened in the name of the Lord our God. They are brought low and fallen, but we are raised up and stand erect. Lord, save the kingdom and hear us on the day when we call for you."

Psalm 126, one of the Gradual psalms, sings of the Book of Esdras, "When the Lord turned about the captivity of Sion, we became as those comforted." And again in 122, "I rejoiced when they said to me, 'we will go up in your gates, O Jerusalem. Jerusalem is built as a city in which each one shares fellowship with the other. To it the tribes go up, the tribes of the Lord as a witness to Israel."

5. The prophetic books are indicated in almost every psalm. Psalm 50 speaks of the coming of the Savior, and that through God, he will come among us. "The Lord will come openly, O our God, and will not keep silence." And in 118, "Blessed is he who comes in the name of the Lord. We have blessed you from the House of the Lord, Lord God, and he has shone upon us." Acknowledging that he who comes is the Word of the Father, Psalm 107 sings, "He sent his Word and healed them, and rescued them from their calamities." For the Coming One and the Word being sent is himself God. And that he is well aware that this same Word is the Son of God, the psalmist sings in 45 in the voice of the Father. "My heart has uttered a good Word"; and in 110 "From the womb, before the Daystar, I have brought you forth." What offspring of the Father could be spoken of other than of his Word and Wisdom? And knowing full well that this is the Word, by whom the Father says "Let there be light," and the firmament and the whole creation (Genesis 1), the same book says "By the Word of the Lord the heavens were established and by the breath of his mouth all their powers" (Psalm 33).

6. Far from being ignorant of the coming of Christ, the psalmist sings particularly about this in 45. "Your throne, O God, is forever and ever, a scepter of righteousness is the scepter of your kingdom. Because you have loved justice and hated injustice, God, your God, has anointed you with the oil of gladness above your companions." And if anyone might think of his coming merely as a kind of phantasm, in Psalm 87 it points to the human birth of him through whom all things were generated. "Mother Sion says, 'a man, a man, indeed, shall be born of her, and the

58

most High, himself, will set her on a firm foundation.'" And this is the same as saying, "and the Word was God," "all things were made through him," "and the Word became flesh" (John 1:1, 3, 14). Because the psalmist knows about his birth from a virgin as well, he does not keep silent about this. On the contrary, he gives an immediate emphasis to this in 45 when he says, "Listen, daughter, and see, and incline your ear, and forget your people and your father's house, for the king has desired your beauty." This is just like what Gabriel said, "Hail, full of grace, the Lord is with you" (Luke 1:28). For the psalmist, having declared him the Christ, immediately proclaims his human birth from the virgin, saying, "Listen, daughter." See how, on the one hand, Gabriel calls Mary by name, being of a different order of creation, while David rightly addresses her as daughter since he is her ancestor.

7. Having spoken of his human birth, the psalmist goes on to show the Word subject to suffering in the flesh. In the second psalm, he sings of what he has seen of the plot devised by the Jews. "Why has the nation raged, and why do the people consider vain things? The kings of the earth have taken their stand, and the leaders have gathered together against the Lord and against his Christ." In Psalm 22 he speaks in the person of the Savior about the manner of his death, "You have brought me to the dust of death for many dogs have encircled me, the assembly of the evildoers has surrounded me. They have dug through my hands and feet, they have numbered all my bones. They have gazed and stared at me. They have divided my clothes among them, and upon my apparel they cast lots." What can "they have dug through my hands and feet" signify except the crucifixion? The psalmist places all these teachings in front of us because the Lord suffered all this not on his own account but for us. In speaking again in the person of the Savior he says in Psalm 88, "Upon me has his anger been laid," and in 69, "What I did not seize, then I paid back in full." For he did not die as one responsible for his own deeds, but he suffered for our sake, and because of our transgressions he bore the weight of the anger that was truly ours; as it is written in the Book of Isaiah, "He took upon himself our weakness" (Isa. 53:4). It also refers to us in Psalm 138, "The Lord will repay on my behalf." And speaking through the Spirit in 72, "And he will save the sons of the poor and will put down the slanderer because the poor man will be delivered from the hands of the oppressor, and the needy one for whom there was no helper."

8. And there is more. Psalm 24 foretells his bodily ascension,

"Lift up your gates, O Rulers, be lifted up, O eternal gates, and the King of Glory will enter in." In 47, "God ascends in the midst of rejoicing, the Lord with trumpet blast." And the psalmist goes on to announce the Savior's being seated in solemnity as he says in Psalm 110, "The Lord said to my Lord. Sit at my right hand until I make your enemies as a footstool for your feet." In Psalm 9, the psalmist loudly proclaims the coming destruction of the devil, "You have been seated on the throne, you who judge righteousness. You have rebuked the nations, and the impious one is destroyed." That he received all judgment from the Father is not concealed; on the contrary, Psalm 72 foretells his coming as judge of all. "O God, give your judgment to the king, and your righteousness to the son of the king to judge the people in righteousness and the poor in justice." In 50, "He will summon the heaven above and the earth that he may pass judgment on his people, and the heavens shall declare his righteousness, that God is judge indeed." And in Psalm 82, "God stands in the assembly of the gods, and in their midst he judges the gods." The calling of the Gentiles can be learnt from many passages in this same book, especially in Psalm 47. "Clap your hands, all you nations, and in triumphant tones shout to God"; and in Psalm 72, "The foes shall fall down before him, and his enemies shall lick the dust. Kings of Tarshis and the islands will bring gifts, and all the kings of the earth will kneel before him and all the nations shall serve him." Everything, then, which is sung in the Psalms is also proclaimed in each of the other books.

9. However, the old man went on to say, I am well aware that, on the other hand, many references to the Savior are given special prominence in every one of the books of the Scriptures, and that what is proclaimed is the one and the same symphony of the Spirit. For just as one can find the themes of all the other books in the Book of the Psalms, so, too, what is special to this book is found often in the rest of the Scriptures; that Moses writes a song, that Isaiah sings, that Habakkuk prays with song and in the same way in every book we see the prophecies, lawmaking, and histories. The same Spirit is over all, and each book ministers and fulfills the grace given to it according to what is apportioned to each by the Spirit whether it be prophecy, lawmaking, the recording of history, or the grace of the psalms, since it is one and the same Spirit, to whom all these diverse gifts belong, and yet who is indivisible by nature. So that while the disclosures accord with the

variety of gifts of the Spirit in relation to the ministry which each enjoys, yet the whole Spirit is in each book. Frequently, then, each one, in dependence on the Spirit, ministers the word as the need arises; thus, as I said before, Moses at one time or another makes laws, prophesies, or sings, and the prophets while engaged in prophetic utterance at times give commands: "Wash, make yourselves clean" (Isa. 1:16); "Wash away the evil from your hearts, Jerusalem." (Jer. 4:14). At other times, they record history, as in the Book of Daniel, we read about Suzanna (Daniel 12), while in the Book of Isaiah, we read of Rab-shekeh and Sennacherib. (Isa. 36:22; 37:21 LXX)

For the Book of the Psalms has the special characteristic of communicating in song what is detailed in prose in the other book, thus rendering with melody this same subject matter but giving it a more general treatment, as I have pointed out. Then, at times this book turns to lawmaking, "Pause from wrath, and forsake anger" (Psalm 37) and, "Turn aside from evil and do good, seek peace and follow after it" (Psalm 34). And, at times it records history such as the journey of Israel, or it prophesies about the Savior, just as I have said before.

10.  Let then the grace of the Spirit be common to all the Scriptures; let it be found in each book individually, and yet the same grace for all, just as the need demands and the Spirit wills. The distribution of the gifts does not reflect the more or the less of this need, but what matters is that each fulfills and perfects its own particular ministry with utmost fidelity. However, the Book of the Psalms possesses a certain grace all of its own and an exceptional quality of perceptiveness. For besides the characteristics it has in common with the other books, it possesses an extraordinary grace peculiar to itself—it reflects the movements of each soul, its vicissitudes and amendments, all represented and portrayed within the book itself. For this reason, anyone who has no bounds to his desire to receive and understand from this book, so as to mold himself, will find it written here. For in the other books you only hear the law commanding what you must do or what act is forbidden; one listens to the prophets only to see the coming of the Savior; one turns to the histories to be able to know of the deeds of the kings and of the saints. But in the book of the Psalms, in addition to listening so that one can learn all this, one contemplates and is instructed about the movements of his own soul; and furthermore, from what he experiences and in what he

is oppressed, again out of this book, he is able to possess the image of the words so that not only when he has listened he may disregard the passion but also he learns what words are necessary and what to do to heal it.

In the other books there are the words prohibiting things that are demeaning but in this book it describes how you ought to abstain from sin; it prescribes what kind of repentance—that repentance is to stop sinning; then, how to repent as well as the very words that must be used in this repentance are to be found in this book. Consider the words of Paul: "Affliction" of the soul "makes for endurance, and endurance for approved virtue, and approval for hope, and hope will not leave us disappointed" (Rom. 5:3–5). In the Psalms we read how afflictions must be borne, and what one should say both during and after the affliction, how every single person is to be tested, and the kind of words for those who are hoping upon the Lord—all this is written and inscribed in the Book of the Psalms. Again, there is the command to give thanks in all circumstances (cf. 1 Thess. 5:16), but the Psalms teach us what words to say when we are giving thanks. Furthermore, when we hear from others, that whoever wishes to live a godly life will suffer persecution (cf. 2 Tim. 3:2), in the Psalms we are given instruction in these matters; we learn what words the fugitive should cry out, and what words are appropriate to offer up to God while you are persecuted and after being rescued. We are instructed to bless the Lord and to confess our praise to him, but in the Psalms we are given a model of how to sing to the Lord and with what words to express fitting praise. Thus for every person whatsoever, we may find the divine songs appropriate for us and for the states of emotional turmoil or stability.

11. In addition, there is further paradox in the Psalms. In the other books, those who are reciting what the saints are saying or what is being said about them are proclaiming what has been written about these holy ones, but the listeners are well aware of themselves as other than the saints about whom the word is spoken; and when certain actions are commanded, the hearers may go so far as in reverence and zeal as to imitate the saints. However, while one may take up in this book the prophecies with regard to the Savior such as are constantly narrated with wonder and reverence in the other Scriptures, in the rest of the psalms, it is as if one's own words were being recited; while those who listen to the words are pierced to the heart and appropriate to themselves

what is expressed in the songs as if the words were their very own.

Taking the example of the blessed Apostle Paul, do not shrink from repeating the same words for the sake of clarity. Many of the words of the patriarchs were spoken as proper to themselves; Moses spoke and God answered. Elijah and Elisha, seated on Mount Carmel, cried out to the Lord and were always proclaiming, "The Lord lives, in whose sight I stand this very day." And while the words of the other holy prophets especially concerned the Savior, yet at times a very great number of prophecies were made to the Gentiles and to Israel. Likewise no one can apply the words of the Patriarchs to themselves alone, nor imitate the commands of Moses and claim the expressions as one's very own, nor those of Abraham concerning the bondwoman and Ishmael, or to appropriate for oneself the words which speak of the greatness of Isaac, even if in the grip of a dire necessity. Not even when compassionating with the suffering, or on occasion being filled with yearning for some better thing, would one dare to make one's own the prayer of Moses, "Show yourself to me" (Exod. 33:13) or again, "If you forgive their sin, then forgive it; if not, blot me out of your book, which you have written." (Exod. 32:32). And neither would anyone take for themselves the words of praise or blame addressed to the prophets, for no one whatsoever could be praised or blamed for deeds such as these. Never could one say, "May the Lord live, in whose presence I stand today!" (1 Kings 17:1) presuming to mouth the words as one's very own. For when one encounters these books it is clear that the words are not one's own, but revelations of the saints of whom the Scriptures speak. On the other hand, the paradox of the psalms is, that except for certain prophecies belonging to the Savior or to Gentiles, in the words expressed by others of themselves, each person sings what has been written as about himself or herself, not at all as if receiving and reciting what was intended for someone else; they take it as their own, as if the words were theirs, and offer it to God as though they had composed the words themselves. For it is not as the expression of the Patriarchs, or Moses, or the other prophets, that these words are reverenced but the ones saying the psalm are confident that these words are their own, and were written on their behalf. Whether they have kept the law or have transgressed, the psalms encompass the deeds of each.

12. It seems to me that the psalms are as a mirror in which you

contemplate yourself and the movements of your soul, and thus confess your understanding of them. And when you listen to what is read, you admit that what is being said in the song is about yourself. Either you are turned to repentance by the piercing of your conscience, or on hearing about the hope one should have towards God and the help extended towards those who become believers, you rejoice in such a grace being granted to you, and begin to give thanks to God. Thus, when you perceive in the third psalm something of your own afflictions, and so consider what is expressed in the psalm to be your own, then in Psalms 12 and 17 you give voice to your own trust and devotion, while the words of Psalm 50 are an expression of your own repentance. So too in 54, 56, 57, and 142, you sing, not as if someone else were being persecuted, but as if it is out of your own experience that you sing to the Lord. In this way, the whole of every Psalm is spoken and composed by the Spirit, so that as was said before in all this, the movements of our souls may be understood. All of them are said about us, and the words are to be assumed as our very own, as a reminder of the movements of the soul, and as an amendment of our daily conduct, and so what has been expressed in the psalms can be for us as models and patterns.

13. Again, the same grace is from the Savior. In becoming man for our sakes, he offered up his own body to death for our sake to redeem all from death, and wishing to show us his own heavenly and pleasing way of living, he made a model of this in himself, lest anyone be deceived easily by the Enemy, such a one having as a pledge of assurance the Savior's victory over the devil for our sake. It was through this example that he not only taught but he performed what he taught, so that while each may listen to him as he speaks, but also, gazing as on an image, may take from him the pattern of conduct as one hears, "Learn from me, that I am gentle and humble of heart" (Matt. 11:29). The most perfect teaching of virtue is not to be found anywhere except where the Lord models it in himself. For whether it is forbearance, or love for humankind, or goodness or courage or mercy, or righteousness, all are to be found in him, and thus there will be nothing lacking in the virtue of the one who closely observes this human life of the Savior. Paul was aware of this when he said, "Become imitators of me, as I am of Christ" (1 Cor. 11:1). The Greeks were gifted as lawmakers, as far as wording the laws, but the Lord, being indeed Lord of all and caring for all his works, not only makes laws, but

gives a model in himself for those who wish to see how they should be performed. Accordingly, even before he came among us, he taught us by the sound of a voice—the voice in the Psalms, so that, just as in this same book he showed the earthly and heavenly man being typified in himself, the person who wishes to be able to observe closely from the psalms the movements and dispositions of the souls will discover in them the remedy and the means of amendment of every movement of the soul.

14. To speak even more to the point, the whole of the divine Scripture is a teacher of virtue and true faith, but the Book of Psalms possesses an image of the way in which souls course through life. Just as someone coming into the presence of a king assumes an appropriate dress and mode of expression, lest lacking these he be rejected as uncouth, in like manner when one tries to make progress in virtue and wishes to contemplate the way of life of the Savior in the body, the divine book first through reading calls to mind the movements of the soul, and thus, in addition, it provides a model for, as well as teaches, those who are making intercession by such words. In order that one may observe this characteristic of the book first, there are psalms spoken in narration, those which admonish, those spoken in prophecy, or in the form of prayer, or confession.

In narrative form, there are Psalms 19, 44, 49, 50, 73, 77, 78, 89, 90, 107, 114, 127, and 137. Those which are in prayer form are 17, 68, 90, 102, 132, and 142. While those which combine intercession, prayer and entreaty are 5, 6, 7, 12, 13, 16, 25, 28, 31, 35, 38, 43, 54, 55, 56, 57, 59, 60, 61, 64, 83, 86, 88, 138, 140, and 143.

A combination of intercession and thanksgiving is found in 138. While intercession alone in found in 3, 26, 69, 70, 71, 74, 79, 80, 109, 123, 130, and 131.

Under the form of a confession we find 9, 75, 92, 105, 106, 108, 111, 118, 136, 138. While the psalms with a combination of confession and narrative form are 9, 75, 106, 107, 118, and 138, confession and narrative are combined with praise as found in 110.

In the form of admonition there is 37; while prophetic material is found in 21, 22, 45, 47, and 76. Proclamation and prophecy is found in 110, encouragement and admonition are found in 33, 39, 81, 95, 96, 97, 98, 103, 104, and 114. Encouragement together with the singing of praise is in 150.

Psalms which describe the life of virtue are 105, 112, 119, 125, and 133. And those devoted to the proclamation of praise are 91, 113, 117, 135, 145, 147, 149, and 150.

Psalms of thanksgiving are 8, 9, 18, 34, 46, 63, 77, 85, 115, 116, 121, 122, 124, 126, 129, and 144. Those which declare a blessing are 1, 32, 41, 119, and 128. And another which is appropriate for expressing steadfastness in song form is 108.

A psalm exhorting to courage is 81, while others which accuse the impious and those who act contrary to the laws are 2, 14, 26, 52, 53.

Words of invocation are found in Psalm 4. And there are psalms proclaiming what is longed for such as 20, and 64, and psalms which proclaim words glorying in the Lord: 23, 27, 39, 40, 42, 62, 76, 84, 97, 99, and 150.

Others such as 58 and 82 put one to shame.

There are special hymn forms, such as Psalms 48 and 65. Psalm 66 rejoices in the resurrection, while we find Psalm 100 but a single expression of jubilation.

15. As I said before, the psalms are composed in such a way that whoever is praying can find the movements and the condition of his own soul and, further, is provided with the model and the instruction for each of these states. You are able to please the Lord in making such expressions your own, to be able to reform yourself, and with the appropriate words give thanks to the Lord lest you fall into impiety. For we have to render an account to the Judge not only for deeds but also for idle words (cf. Matt. 12:36). Consider the following—

If you wish to declare someone blessed, you learn how to do so and whom to call upon and the words to say in Psalms 1, 32, 41, 112, 119, 128. When finding fault with the conspiracy of the Jews against the Savior you have Psalm 2. If persecuted by your own people, and you have a whole crowd against you, say Psalm 3. And if after being deeply troubled, you cried out to the Lord and your prayer was heard and now you wish to give thanks, sing Psalm 4, 75, or 115.

When you see the evildoers planning to lie in wait for you, and you wish your prayer to be heard, get up at dawn and say Psalm 5. When you feel the Lord's displeasure, if you see that you are troubled by this, you can say Psalms 6 and 38. When certain people plot against you, as did Achitophel against David, and you are informed of this, sing Psalm 7 and place your trust in God who will deliver you.

16. As you see the grace of the Savior extended everywhere, the human race being saved, if you wish to raise your voice to the Lord, sing Psalm 8; or you can use the same psalm as well as 84 in thanksgiving for the vintage harvest.

When the enemy is being accused, and creation saved, do not take the glory for yourself, but know that this is the victory of the Son of God and sing to him in the words of Psalm 9.

If anyone wishes to disturb you, hold on strongly to your confidence in the Lord and say Psalm 10.

When you see the arrogance of the crowd and evil spreading everywhere so that there seems to be no one left who is pleasing to God, take refuge in the Lord and say Psalm 12. And though the plot of the enemies lasts a very long time, do not lose heart, as though God had forgotten you, but call upon the Lord, singing Psalm 13.

When you hear some people blaspheming against the providence of God, do not make common cause with them in their impiety, but on the other hand, intercede with God, saying Psalms 14 and 53; and, what is more, if you wish to learn what sort of person is a citizen of the kingdom of heaven, sing Psalm 15.

17. When you are in difficulty as enemies circle around you threatening your life, say Psalms 17, 86, 88, and 141; or if you wish to learn how Moses prayed, you have 90. However, when you have been saved from your enemies, and delivered from your pursuers, sing Psalm 18.

As you wonder at the order of creation, the grace of providence and the sacred prescriptions of the Law, sing Psalms 19 and 24.

When you see others in affliction, comfort them by praying with them in the words of Psalm 20.

When you see yourself shepherded and guided safely by the Lord, rejoice in the words of Psalm 23.

When enemies surround you, lift up your soul to God in Psalm 25, and you will see these evildoers put to flight; but if these persist, and, with hands red with blood, try to drag you down and kill you, remember that God is the proper judge (for he alone is righteous while that which is human is limited) and so say the words of 26, 35, and 43.

If you experience the harsh and vehement attacks of the enemy, and they crowd against you, despising you as one who is not anointed (cf. LXX heading), and on this very account they fight against you, do not succumb to these attacks but sing Psalm 27.

And if you suffer from the weakness of nature as the plots

against you grow more shameless so that you have scarcely any rest, then cry out to the Lord, in Psalm 28.

If in a spirit of gratitude you wish to teach how one should make a spiritual offering to the Lord, sing Psalm 29.

And furthermore, in dedicating (cf. LXX heading) your house—that is your soul which welcomes the Lord, and the bodily house in which you dwell corporeally—rejoice and sing Psalm 30 and Psalm 127 from the Gradual psalms.

18. When you see yourself hated and persecuted by all your relatives and friends because of the truth, do not be downcast either for them or for yourself; and when all your acquaintances turn away from you, do not be frightened, but withdraw from them and keep your eyes fixed on the future, singing Psalm 31.

Or when you see people being ransomed and baptized out of a generation that is perishing, and you are in wonder at the loving-kindness of God towards the human race, then sing to them Psalm 32.

When you are gathered together with people who are righteous and upright of life, sing with them Psalm 33.

Or if you have chanced upon enemies and yet have prudently fled from them and their schemes, call together people of gentle disposition and give thanks in the words of Psalm 34.

When you see transgressors of the law being so zealous in their evildoing, do not attribute this evil to nature—this is what the heretics teach—but in saying Psalm 36 know that they are the cause of their own sinful behavior.

If, when those evil and lawless people are opposing the lowly, and you wish to admonish the latter not to pay attention or to be provoked to envy—since such evildoers will speedily be destroyed—say to yourself and to the others Psalm 37.

19. If, on the other hand, you wish to pray on your own behalf as the enemy prepares the attacks, there is all the more reason, in arming yourself for the battle, to sing the words of Psalm 39; and during the attack, as you suffer the afflictions, and wish to learn the advantage of steadfast patience, sing 40.

When many are poor and needy and you wish to show pity for them, on the one hand acknowledging the generosity of some people, and urging others on to similar deeds of mercy, say Psalm 41.

If in your intense longing for God, you hear the reviling of your enemies, do not give way to fear, but know that such a longing bears an immortal fruit, and comfort your soul with hope in God. When you are uplifted by this, and earthly sorrow has been assuaged a little, say Psalm 42.

If you wish to call to mind constantly the benefits of God to the Patriarchs, the exodus out of Egypt, the passage through the desert, and how while God is so good, human beings are ungrateful, you have Psalms 44, 78, 89, 105, 106, 107, and 114.

When you have fled to God for refuge and are delivered from the afflictions round about you, if you wish to give thanks to God and to recount his kindness toward you, you have Psalm 46.

20. But after you have sinned and then in shame have repented and have pleaded for mercy, you have words of both confession and conversion in Psalm 51.

When you have been slandered before an evil king, and you see the slanderer boasting of his deeds, withdraw and say Psalm 52.

When you are persecuted and have been handed over to the slanderers, who intend what the Ziphites and the heathen did to David (1 Sam. 23:19–24) and do not lose heart but call upon the Lord, and sing hymns to him in 54 and 55.

And even if the one who pursues you closely unknowingly enters the very cave in which you are hiding (cf. 1 Sam. 24:3), do not fear, for you have oracles for such an extremity and words of consolation inscribed for you in Psalms 56 and 141.

When the enemies rush violently toward you, thinking to kill you, submit to God, placing your confidence on him. The more they rage, the greater should be your obedience to the Lord in the words of Psalm 62.

If in being persecuted you flee to the desert, do not fear being alone in that place, because God is there. So rise early in the morning and sing Psalm 63.

And when you are in fear of the enemies who never cease to lie in wait but are constantly searching for you, do not yield in the slightest degree even when they are so numerous. Their blows will be as the darts with which children play. Then sing Psalms 64, 65, 70, and 71.

21. When you wish to sing praise to the Lord, you have Psalm 65; if you wish to teach about the resurrection, Psalm 66; and when you ask for pity from God, sing praise to him in Psalm 67.

When you see the impious in peace and prosperity living just as they wish, while the just are in affliction, sing Psalm 73, lest you be scandalized and severely shaken.

And when God is angry against the people, you have the prudent words of Psalm 74 as a consolation; when it is necessary to give full confession sing Psalms 9, 75, 92, 105, 106, 107, 108, 111, 118, 126, and 138.

When you wish the Greeks and heretics to be put to shame, since the knowledge of God is not found among them, but only in the catholic church, then sing Psalm 76.

When the enemies seize even the places of refuge, and you are afflicted on all sides and are deeply troubled, do not give up in despair, but pray; and when your prayer is heard give thanks to God in Psalm 77.

And if the enemies persist in profaning the house of God and kill the saints and even expose the bodies to birds of the air, draw together compassionately with those who suffer, do not be overwhelmed with terror, but plead to God saying Psalm 79.

22. And on the feast day, when you wish to sing praise to the Lord, call together the servants of God, and you have Psalms 81 and 95. And then, when once more the enemies surround you on all sides, threatening the house of God and making common cause against the God-fearing, do not be frightened by their numbers or their power, but hold on to the words of Psalm 83, as to an anchor of hope. If in beholding the house of God, and his eternal tabernacle, you experience an intense longing such as the Apostle had, you have the words of Psalm 84. When, at length, the anger has abated, and you are released from captivity, if you wish to give thanks, you have the words of Psalms 85 and 126. If you wish to discover the difference between the catholic and the schismatic churches, and so confound the latter, you can sing Psalm 6. And to encourage yourself and others in the fear of the Lord, and since hope in God is never put to shame but prepares the soul in fearlessness, sing to God in the words of Psalm 91. Do you wish to give thanks on the Sabbath? You have Psalm 92 (LXX heading).

23. Do you wish to give thanks on the Lord's Day? You have Psalm 24. If on the second day of the week, then Psalm 48. If you wish to give praise on the Day of Preparation you have Psalm 93. For this was the time of the crucifixion when the house of the Lord was built in spite of the attempts of the enemies to prevent this. And it is on account of this victory it is fitting to sing this psalm. But when, after being captured, the house was torn down and then later rebuilt, you have the words of Psalm 96 (LXX heading). When the land is at peace and enjoys the reestablishment after war and is under the dominion of the Lord, if you wish to

sing of these circumstances, you have Psalm 97. Do you wish to sing on the fourth day of the week? You have Psalm 94. For it was on this day that the Lord was betrayed and thus moved toward the penalty of death and so made retribution. It was on this day, too, that he triumphed openly, since if you read the Gospels you see that it was the fourth day of the week when the Jews plotted against him, and that he boldly confronted the devil on our account; so sing Psalm 94.

When you see the dominion and providence of God in all things, and you wish to instruct others in faith and obedience to him, then persuade them first to a confession of praise in Psalm 100.

And when you learn his power of judging, and yet, since the Lord judges, it is justice and mercy mixed together, then, in your approach to him, you have the words of Psalm 101.

24. Since our nature is weak, if you are oppressed by the anguish of life, then you have comfort for your weariness in Psalm 102.

And since it is fitting for us to give thanks to God through all and in all things, when you wish to praise him, you have Psalms 103 and 104 for the encouragement of your soul.

Do you wish to sing to God and to know how to sing and in what circumstances, and what is to be fittingly praised? You have 105, 107, 135, 147, 148, 149, and 150.

Do you have faith, as the Lord says, and do you believe in the prayers you say? Then say 116.

But do you perceive that through your actions you are making progress, but say with Paul, that you "forget the things that lie behind, and press on to that which is ahead"? You have the fifteen Gradual psalms for every step of the way.

25. But, if you were being captivated by alien thoughts, and you perceive yourself being misled, but although repenting and intending to desist for the future yet you remain near those who overcame you when you were sinning—then, sit down and indeed weep as did the people saying Psalm 137. And after being tested by temptations, if you wish to give thanks you have Psalm 139, and when again you may be hard pressed by the enemies and you wish to escape, you have Psalm 140.

Do you wish to entreat in prayer? Sing Psalms 5 and 143.

When a tyrant rises up against you and the people, as Goliath against David, do not fear, but trust as David did, and say Psalm 144.

When you consider with wonder all the benevolence of God,

recalling all that he has done for you and for everyone, to give praise to God on this account say the words of David himself, in Psalm 145. Do you wish to sing praise to the Lord? You have the words of Psalms 93 and 98.

If, in spite of your insignificance, you are elected to a position of authority among your brethren, do not put on airs among them, but give the glory to God who chose you and sing David's own words in Psalm 150 (LXX final psalm).

But if you wish to sing those psalms especially designated as Alleluia hymns—you have 105, 106, 107, 112, 113, 114, 115, 116, 117, 118, 119, 135, 136, 146, 147, 148, 149, and 150.

26. When you wish to sing something especially devoted to the Savior, you will find that such references are in almost every single psalm. However, in Psalms 45 and 110, you will find special revelations of his generation from the Father and his coming in the flesh. In Psalms 22 and 69, there are predictions about the divine cross and about the kind of plots he accepted on our behalf; and again Psalms 2 and 109 indicate the plotting and wickedness of the Jews, and the betrayal by Judas Iscariot. Psalms 21, 50, and 72 reveal his kingdom, and the power of his judgment, and his coming again in the flesh to us, and the summoning of the nations. Psalm 16 reveals his resurrection from the dead, while 24 and 47 announce his ascension into heaven. And when you read Psalms 93, 96, 98, and 99 you can contemplate the benefits made for us by the Savior through his Passion.

27. In such a way, then, is the character of the assistance afforded to humankind by the Book of Psalms, which contains some psalms having distinctive qualities of their own while in others one can find very frequently prophecies of the coming in the body of our Lord and Savior Jesus Christ, as I said before.

At this point, it is very necessary not to pass over the reasons why words of this kind are to be intoned with melody and song. For there are certain rather simplistic people among us who, while they believe that the words are divinely inspired, yet consider that the psalms have been put to music merely for the pleasure of the listener. But this is not the case. For Scripture does not seek just for sweetness or elegance for its own sake, but rather it is composed in such a way to be of benefit for the soul. There are two reasons in particular. First, it is fitting that the divine Scripture praises God not only in the single tone of prose, but also by the whole range of the voice. While prose tone is suited to the recitation of the law and the prophets and all the histories together with the New Testament, on the other hand it is appropriate to give expression to the psalms, the odes, and the canticles with the whole range of the voice just as we are to find salvation by loving God with the whole of our strength and power. The second reason is this: just as the concord of sound of flutes played together results in a harmonious unity, so, too, when the various movements of the soul are recognized, that is the reasoning faculties, and the desire and the passions in the soul, and the activity of the members of the body originating in these movements, the reason does not wish that a man be in disharmony with himself, nor be alienated from himself. Consequently, it is best to act according to reason, but worst is to act according to the passions. This is what Pilate did when he said, "I find no cause in him" (John 18:38), while at the same time concurring in the decision of the Jews. It is to commit evil through desire, if unable to sin through deed, as did the old men in the story about Suzanna. Or to give further examples, not to commit fornication, but to steal; or the contrary, to abstain from stealing, while committing murder; or again to abstain from murder while committing blasphemy.

28. Lest any disturbance of this kind occur in us, reason wishes the soul to have the mind of Christ, as the apostle Paul says (1 Cor. 2:16), to take advantage of this guide, and by it to take hold of the faculties of sensation in the soul, and to direct the members of the body towards obedience to reason. As a plectrum in music, so one becomes a harp, wholly attentive to the Spirit, that one may obey through all the members of the body and the movements of the soul, and may serve the will of God.

The harmonious recitation of the psalms is an image and a model of this kind of calmness and tranquility of the faculties of reason. For just as we make the thoughts of the soul known and we communicate through the utterance of words, so, too, the Lord, wishing the melody of the words to be a symbol of the spiritual harmony in the soul, has ordained that the odes be sung harmoniously and the psalms be recited with song. And this is the longing of the souls that it be well disposed, as the Scriptures say, "Are any among you in good spirits? Then sing" (James 5:13).

In this way by our singing the psalms, whatever is disordered and rough and undisciplined in the soul is calmed and grief healed. "Why are you sad, my soul, and do you disturb me?"

(Psalms 42 and 43) And our stumbling is acknowledged when we say "My feet were almost tottering" (Psalm 73), while fear is overwhelmed by hope in the words "The Lord is my helper, I shall not fear whatever man may do to me" (Psalm 118).

29. Those who do not recite the sacred odes this way do not sing wisely but rather just for pleasure. While they delight themselves, they are blameworthy because "songs of praise are not to be on the lips of sinners" (Sir. 15:9). On the other hand, those who sing the psalms in the way I have previously discussed, bring the melody arising from the rhythm of the soul in accord with the symphony with the Spirit. In this way, those who sing with the tongue and sing with the mind (cf. 1 Cor. 14:15) not only have great benefit for themselves but also for those who wish to listen to them. For the blessed David singing thus for Saul was himself pleasing to God and drove the disturbed and mad passion out of Saul and prepared his soul for tranquility. In this way, the singing of the priests invoked calmness upon the souls of the people so that they would be of one mind with those of the heavenly choirs.

So then to recite the psalms melodiously is not to seek the mere pleasure of sound but rather it is to give outward expression to the harmony of the reasoning faculties in the soul. And the melodious recitation is a symbol of the rhythmical and tranquil restoration of the understanding. For the praises to God on well-sounding cymbals, the cithara, and the ten-stringed harp again symbolize the natural concord of the members of the body like the harp strings, while the reasoning faculties of the soul become like cymbals. Furthermore by the sound and by the command of the Spirit all these move and live. As it is written, "By the Spirit, man lives and puts to death the deeds of the body" (Rom. 8:13).

Thus he who sings well puts his soul in order and so leads what is of unbalanced rhythm to an equilibrium, so that being established in its proper nature, it may fear nothing, and in freedom from phantoms of the future, it may direct itself to longing for the good things to come. For by the rhythmic melody, the soul is well ordered and forgets its passions, and fixing its gaze upon that mind in Christ (1 Cor. 2:16), it concentrates its faculties on that which is the most excellent.

30. It is necessary, my child, that everyone coming to this book read it with sincerity since the whole of it is inspired by God; and

then select from it, as from the fruits of a blessed garden, what is useful as the need is perceived. For it is my opinion that the whole experience of human life, the disposition of the soul, and the movements of the reasoning faculties are encompassed in the words of this book, and that nothing outside of this is found in human life. For whether there is a need for repentance or confession of praise, or for help in affliction or temptation, or any kind of persecution; whether someone was freed from plotting or if someone was saddened and disturbed on some account or was suffering in some way by what is described above; or if he sees himself advancing, while the enemy is set aside, he may wish to praise and thank and bless the Lord—in all these circumstances he has instructions in the divine psalms; let him choose from among all these expressions, which have been written as his own and, according to that wording, offer them to the Lord.

31. However, do not encrust these words with any extraneous and rhetorical expressions or attempt to change the words or introduce any form of variation whatsoever, but say and sing what is written without artifice of any kind—just as it was expressed—so that the righteous men who gave them to us will recognize them as their own and will pray with us. Furthermore, the Spirit who spoke through these saints, perceiving his own words being sounded with these, will come to our aid. For just as the lives of the saints are better than that of others, so too their words are better and more efficacious than ours, if someone were to speak truthfully. For in these words they were pleasing to God, and in saying them, as the Apostle said, "They overcame kingdoms, enforced justice, obtained promises, stopped the mouths of lions, quenched mighty fires, escaped the edge of the sword, from weakness came to strength, became mighty in battle, routed foreign armies, and women received back their dead through resurrection" (Heb. 11:33–35).

32. Therefore let everyone now who recites the psalms have confidence that through these words God will quickly give ear to those who are in need. For if someone saying this is in affliction, he finds great consolation in them. If the one singing the psalm is being tested and persecuted, he will appear more approved and be taken under the protection of the Lord who defended the one who composed these words. And, in these words he will put to flight the devil and frighten off his demons. And when he says these words, if he has sinned, he will be ashamed of himself and

stop sinning; but if he has not sinned, he will find himself rejoicing that he is straining eagerly toward that which lies ahead, and thus entering into the fray in the strength of the Psalms, he will never waver from the truth. But he will reprove those who deceive and attempt trickery; and this rests not on any human guarantor, but on the divine Scripture itself. For God commanded Moses to write a splendid song and to teach the people; and he ordered the one appointed as leader to write Deuteronomy, to have this in his hands, and to always meditate upon its words (Deut. 19:18), since these words are sufficient in themselves both to recall virtue to the mind and to bring assistance to the one who meditates upon them in sincerity. When Joshua, the son of Nun, entered the land, he saw the enemy drawn up in battle formation and the kings of the Amorites assembling to give battle. In the face of all these shields and weapons he read aloud from Deuteronomy in the ears of all and reminded them of the words of the Law, and having thus armed the people, he prevailed over the enemy. King Josiah, too, when he found the book and it had been read aloud for all to hear, no longer feared the enemy. And, at any time when there was a war against the people, the ark which contained the tablets of the Law was carried before the whole army and was sufficient assistance against any battle formation—unless among its bearers there were any prevailing hypocrisy or sinfulness in the people, because faith and a sincere disposition are necessary for the Law to work in conjunction with prayer.

33. And I have heard, said the old man, from wise men how in Israel in the old days in the simple reading aloud of Scriptures demons were put to flight, and in the same way, their plots against humankind were exposed. For this reason he said that those deserved condemnation who neglected the words of Scripture, while using persuasive expressions from alien sources and employing these in forms of exorcisms. Rather, they were merely amusing themselves and offering themselves to the ridicule of the demons. How the Jews, the sons of Sceva, suffered when they tried to exorcise the person in this way! (Acts 29:14–16). The demons when they heard such words were amused, but they were afraid of the words of holy men, and they could not endure them. For the Lord himself is in the words of Scripture, and it is him whom they cannot endure: "I beg you, do not torment me before the time" (Luke 8:28). And thus they were being destroyed only seeing the Lord present. In the same way, Paul commanded

the unclean spirits (Acts 16:18) and the demons were subject to the disciples (Luke 12:17); the hand of the Lord was upon Elisha, the prophet, when he prophesied about the waters to the three kings (2 Kings 3:15) and when the psalmist played at the Lord's bidding.

So it is with us today. If anyone is concerned for the suffering let him use these words and he will help the sufferers more, and at the same time show his own faith to be firm and true, and God, perceiving this, will grant healing to the sufferers in their needs. This the holy one recognizes when he says in Psalm 119, "I meditate upon your righteousness, and I will not forget your words." And again, "Your righteousness was my song of praise in the place of exile." And in these words they worked out their salvation, saying, "If the Law had not been my meditation, then I would have perished in my abasement" (Psalm 119). And for this reason Paul reassured his disciples saying, "Meditate on these things, and remain steadfast in this and your advance be manifest" (1 Tim. 4:15). And so, you, too, meditating on the psalms and making them your own are able to grasp their proper meaning in every one, under the Spirit. Thus you will strive after the manner of life of those holy God-fearing men who have here spoken.

# VI.

## Gregory of Nazianzus

### SERMON 38

(1) Christ is born, give glory to him;
Christ comes from the heavens, gather to meet him;
Christ comes upon the earth, be filled with rejoicing.
"Sing to the Lord, all the earth" [Ps. 96:1]
and, that both heaven and earth are drawn together I say,
"Let the heavens be glad, and the earth rejoice" [Ps. 96:11].
Through the heavenly and then the earthly spheres
Christ is in the flesh;
exult with trembling and with joy—
with trembling, because of sin,
with joy, because of hope.
Christ is come of a virgin,
Women, remain virgins
so that you may become mothers of Christ.
Who would not adore him who is from the beginning?
Who would not give praise to him who is the end of all?

(2) Once more the darkness is dispelled;
Once more the light is exalted;
Once more Egypt is punished by darkness;
Once more Israel is illumined by a pillar of fire.
Let the people sitting in the darkness of ignorance
see a great light of knowledge.
The old has passed away;
behold all things have been made new [2 Cor. 5:17].
The letter withdraws, the Spirit advances;
the shadows flee, the truth breaks in.
Melchizedek is summed up; the motherless becomes father-
less.

First without a mother.
Secondly without a father.
The laws of nature are abrogated
that the cosmos above be brought to perfection.
Christ urges us, let us not resist;
All you nations clap your hands [Ps. 47:1]
because a child is born to us, a son is given to us.
Sovereignty is upon his shoulder (for he was raised up by the
   cross),
and his name is called Mighty Counsellor (of the Father),
Angel [cf. Isa. 10:6].
Let John cry out, "Prepare the way of the Lord" [Matt. 3:3].
I, too, shall proclaim the power of the day.
The One without flesh has assumed flesh;
The Word has taken on materiality;
The Invisible had become visible;
The Impalpable is able to be touched;
The Timeless takes on a beginning;
The Son of God becomes Son of Man,
Jesus Christ,
He who is yesterday, today and forever [Heb. 13:8].
Let the Jews be scandalized,
let the Greeks mock,
let the heretics blaspheme.
At last they will come to believe
when they see him ascending the heavens,
or, at least, at the time when he comes
from the heavens taking his seat as judge.

. . . . . . . . . . . . . .

(17) And now with me welcome the conception,
   and leap for joy, if not like John, in the womb,
   then like David before the resting place of the ark [cf. 2 Sam.
      6:14].
   And sing praise for the census
   through which you are enrolled in the heavens.
   Revere the birth
   through which you are released from the fetters of birth.
   Honor little Bethlehem which leads you back to paradise.
   Adore the manger, through it, you who
   are lacking in reasonableness, are nourished by the Word
      (Reason).

Like the ox, recognize your owner—so Isaiah encourages
   you—
and, like the ass, the manger of its lord [cf. Isa. 1:3].
Either you are one of the purified, subject to the Laws,
ruminating upon right reason
and fit for the offering of the sacrifice,
or you are as yet unfit for the food and the sacrifice
and are still part of the heathen.
Hasten after the star, and offer gifts with the Magi,
gold, incense and myrrh; offer them to Christ
as king, the gold; as him who died for you, the myrrh.
With the shepherds give glory, with the angels hymn praise,
join the choir of the archangels.
May there be common festivities in the powers of heaven
   and earth.
I am convinced that the latter will join in the rejoicing
and the festive making today if indeed they are of good will
towards God and humankind,
like those whom David conducts after the Passion of Christ.
They mount upwards, encouraging
one another to lift up the portals [cf. Ps. 24:7–9].

(18) You are to detest only one aspect of the birth of Christ,
the massacre of the infants ordered by Herod.
Deplore this, the sacrifice of the children of the same age as
   Christ;
they were sacrificed on behalf of the victim of the new age.
And when Christ flees to Egypt, call him out of Egypt,
rightly adoring him in that place.
As the disciple of Christ,
pass blamelessly through all the stages of the life
and growing strength of Christ.
Be purified, circumcised, tear away the veil
surrounding you from your birth.
Then teach in the temple
and drive from the holy place the temple traders.
Suffer to be stoned, if it is necessary;
you will escape the stoners, I assure you,
and you shall flee through their midst, as God did,
for the Word is not to be stoned.
And if you are led before Herod, make little response.
He will be more shamed by your silence than by the wordi-
   ness of others.

And if you are scourged, seek for what is still wanting.
Taste the gall for its bitterness;
don the scarlet robe, grasp the reed,
endure the worship of those who mock the truth.
Finally allow yourself to be crucified, put to death, buried,
so that you may rise with him,
be glorified with him,
reign with him;
and seeing God as he is, and being seen by him;
him who is adored and glorified in the Trinity,
him who is now to be made manifest to us,
him who is made accessible by the bonds of the flesh;
we pray
in Jesus Christ our Lord
to whom is the glory forever. Amen.

# VII.

## Ambrose of Milan

### CONCERNING VIRGINS

1. If, according to the maxim of heavenly truth, we have to render an account of every idle word uttered (cf. Matt. 2:36), or if, like the timid investor or the greedy hoarder, every servant who was entrusted with a large sum of spiritual grace and then hid it in the earth will incur no little blame on the master's return—since it was to have been distributed among the moneylenders, and so be multiplied by the increase of interest payments (cf. Matt. 25:14–30); then, very rightly have we grounds for fear lest a return be demanded for our gift of speech, we, to whom has been allowed a modicum of ability, yet having a pressing necessity to lend out to the minds of the people, the eloquence of God entrusted to us; especially since the Lord requires of us the effort rather than the accomplishment. So I commit this discourse to writing since there is a greater danger to modesty in being listened to, than in being read. A book does not blush.

2. So, diffident of my ability, yet encouraged by the instances of divine mercy, I dare to compose a discourse; for when God so willed, even an ass spoke (Num. 22:28). But if an angel may assist me, who am weighed beneath the burdens of the world, I shall loosen my tongue, long dumb. For he who removed the impediments of nature for the ass, is able to release me from the hindrance of inexperience. In the ark of the Old Testament the rod of the priest blossomed (Num. 17:23). For God it is easy to cause a flower to spring from our gnarled wood, too. And why should we lose heart that the Lord who spoke in the thornbushes should speak in men (Exod. 3:4)? God did not disdain the bush; would that he might illumine my thorns too! Perhaps there will be some who may wonder that, even in our thorns, some brightness

shines; there will be some who at the sound of our voice from the bush, will take off their shoes so that the progress of the mind be freed from bodily impediments.

3.  But such things are merited by holy men. Would that Jesus would cast a glance at me lying under that still barren fig tree, and that after three years my fig tree bear fruit! (Luke 13:6–9). But how should sinners have such hope? If only the vinedresser spoken of in the Lord's gospel—perhaps already ordered to cut down my fig tree—would spare it for this year as well, until he dig around and manure the soil, and so perhaps raise the helpless from the dust and lift the poor out of the mire (Ps. 113:7). Blessed are they who tie up their horses under the vine and the olive (Gen. 44:11), and consecrate the course of their labor to light and joy. Yet I am that fig tree—low in height, brittle in working, soft in use, and barren in fruit—that is to say that the enticement of the pleasures of the world still overshadows me.

4.  And perhaps someone may wonder why I, who am unable to speak, dare to write. And yet, if we recall what we read in the writings of the gospel, with the deeds of the priests and the holy prophet Zachariah as an example for us, one will discover that what the voice cannot explain, the pen can write. But if the name, John, restored his father's voice, then I who am mute ought not to despair of receiving speech, if I speak of Christ of whose generation, the prophet asks who shall declare (Isa. 53:8). And so as a servant I shall proclaim the family of the Lord, for the immaculate Lord has consecrated for himself an immaculate family even out of this body full of human frailty.

5.  It is fortunate that since today is the birthday of a virgin it is about virgins that we speak, and that my book takes its beginning on a note of praise. It is the birthday of a virgin, let us strive for purity. It is the birthday of a martyr, let us offer up sacrifices. It is the birthday of holy Agnes; let men wonder, let children be encouraged, let the married be astounded, let the unmarried imitate. But what can we say that is worthy of her whose very name (cf. Rev. 5:6; 6:9) was not devoid of the light of praise? Her devotion was beyond her years, and her virtue beyond nature, so that it seems to me that her name was not so much that of a human being, as a prophetic declaration of the martyrdom by which she indicated what she was to be.

6.  But I have something which gives me help. The name of virgin is a title of modesty. I shall call upon the martyr, I shall

proclaim the virgin. The words of praise that are not sought for, but those already to hand are elaborate enough. Let us desist from labors of talent, let eloquence be silent, a single word is fitting praise; and this is sung by old men, young people, and children. No one is more deserving of praise than the one praised by all. There are as many heralds speaking her praise as there are those who proclaim her martyr.

7. Tradition tells us that she suffered martyrdom at the age of twelve. The more hateful the cruelty which did not spare such tender years, the greater the strength of faith which was witnessed to even at that age. Was there room for a wound in that little body? And yet she who scarcely had room enough for the blow of the sword had that which conquered the iron. Girls of that age cannot bear an angry expression in their parents' faces. They are likely to weep, as if wounded, at the prick of a needle. But she, dauntless in the cruel hands of the executioner, is unmoved by the dragging weight of the clanking chains. As yet unacquainted with death, yet prepared for it, now she offers her whole body to the sword of the furious soldier. Or again, if hurried against her will to the altars of sacrifice, she stretches out her hands to Christ in the middle of the fire and at those very sacrilegious fires makes the sign of the Lord's trophy of victory. Now she places both hands and neck into iron bands, but no band could enclose such tender limbs.

8. A new kind of martyr! Not yet liable for punishment, yet already mature for victory: To enter the conflict poses a difficulty, to be crowned is easy. She who was disadvantaged by her youth, yet discharged the office of the teaching of virtue. A bride would not hasten to the marriage bed with as joyful step as the virgin went forward to the place of punishment, her head not adorned with plaited hair but with Christ, not bound with dainty flowers but with strength of character. When all were weeping, she alone was dry-eyed. All wondered that she was so readily prodigal of her life—the cup of life barely tasted, and yet relinquished as if already drained. There was universal amazement that here was one ready to testify to the divinity and not yet of an age to testify on her own behalf. And so it was that she succeeded in having her testimony about God believed, for what is beyond nature is from the author of nature.

9. With what terrors the executioner strove to make her afraid, with what blandishments he tried to persuade her! What prom-

ises of marriage were advanced! But she responded, "It would be an injustice to my Spouse to look upon another as being able to please. He who first chose me for himself shall receive me. Executioner, why do you delay? Let the body perish which can be loved by eyes which I refuse." She stood, she prayed, she bent her neck. You could have seen the executioner tremble as if he himself had been condemned; you could have seen his right hand shaking, his face paling as he feared for the danger to someone else, when the girl feared not for herself. You have, then, in one victim, a double martyrdom, for modesty and for religion. She remains a virgin and obtains martyrdom.

10. Now the love of purity urges me and you, my holy, sister, though quiet in your silent custom, to say something of virginity lest it seems that what is its principal virtue is belittled by only a passing reference. For virginity is praiseworthy not because it is found in martyrs but because it itself makes martyrs.

11. Who with human intelligence can comprehend what nature does not include in its laws? Or who with natural language express what is beyond the course of nature? Virginity has been brought from heaven that it might be imitated on earth, and surely it is fitting that she who found for herself a spouse in heaven, should have sought for herself a life style from heaven. Passing beyond the clouds, the air, the angels and the stars, she found the Word of God in the very bosom of the Father and drew him with her whole heart. For who having found so great a good would relinquish it? "For thy name is as perfume poured out; therefore have young maidens loved you and have drawn you" (Song of Sol. 1:1). Finally, this is not some notion of my own, because they who marry not nor are given in marriage are as the angels in heaven (cf. Matt. 22:30). Let no one wonder if they are compared with the angels who are joined with the Lord of the angels. Who then would deny that this style of life which we do not easily find on earth except when God descended into the members of an earthly body has its source in heaven? Then a virgin conceived and the Word became flesh (John 1:14) that flesh might become God.

12. Someone may point out that Elijah did not experience carnal intercourse and therefore he was carried up to heaven by a chariot and so appeared with the Lord in the glory (Matt. 17:3), so he will come as the precursor of the advent of the Lord (Mal. 3:24). And Miriam, taking up the timbrel, led the dancers with

virginal modesty. But consider of what she was the representation. Was it not the church who with immaculate spirit joins together the assemblies of religious people who sing the divine songs? And also we read that at the temple in Jerusalem there were virgins appointed; now what does the apostle say, "These things happened to them in a figure that they might be a sign of the future" (cf. 1 Cor. 10:11). For the figure is in few, but the reality in many.

13. Truly, after the Lord came into the body and fused into one a fellowship of divinity and of body unstained by confusion or mixture, then it was that this heavenly way of life was implanted in human bodies, spread through the whole world. This is what the angels ministering on earth revealed as a race which was to come, which would offer to the Lord ministry by the sacrifice of an immaculate body. This is the ministry which the host of angels singing praise promised on earth. Therefore we have the authority of ancient times and the fullness of the declaration in Christ.

14. Certainly this is not something we have in common with the pagans, nor is it widespread among the barbarians, nor is it practiced among the other animals. With them we enjoy one and the same vital breath of air; we share the same earthly condition of the body, the same mode of generation; yet in this matter alone we deny a natural parallel—because virginity is simulated by the pagans, for when it is consecrated, it is violated; it is attacked by the barbarians and is unknown by the rest.

15. Who will quote the instance of the vestal virgins and the priests of Palas? This kind is more a modesty with regard to time rather than moral character, because it is not perpetual but for a span of years! It is the kind of innocence that is all the more wanton for keeping its corruption for the later life. They themselves, who prescribe a limit to virginity, teach that their virgins neither can nor ought to persevere. What kind of religion is it that bids young girls to modesty and old women to wantonness? But she is not modest whom the law restrains, nor immodest who is released by law. What mystery! What words! Where the necessity of chastity is imposed, and authorization is given to lust. For she is not chaste who is restrained by fear, not honorable who is hired for a price. Nor is that modesty which, exposed daily to the importunity of lustful eyes, is plagued by shameless gazing. Prices are offered and immunities conferred as though it were not the greatest impudence to sell one's chastity. What is promised

for a price is surrendered for a price, it is brought forward for a price, is reckoned at a price. She who is accustomed to sell chastity, does not know how to redeem it.

16.  What shall I say about the Phrygian rites in which immodesty is the rule—and would that it were not so of the weaker sex! What of the orgies of Bacchus where the mystery of the religious rites is an incentive to lust? What of the life style of the priests when the immorality of the gods is worshiped? It is clear that these rites do not possess sacred virgins.

17.  Let us see perhaps if the precepts of philosophy have formed any virgins, for such precepts are accustomed to make claim for themselves as authoritative instruction in all the virtues. There is a story celebrating a certain Pythagorean virgin. When a tyrant was trying to force her to reveal a secret, lest it could be dragged out of her by torture, she bit off her tongue and spat it out in the tyrant's face. Thus he who would not put to an end the questioning, would have nothing to question.

18.  But the same virgin with steadfast soul but swollen womb, an example of speechlessness but a lax discharge of chastity, was conquered by passion, she who was not able to be conquered by torments. And so she who could conceal the secret of the mind did not conceal the shame of the body. She overcame nature but did not observe discipline. How she would wish the defense of her modesty to reside in her speech! Perhaps philosophy taught her to endure suffering so that she might deny her guilt. Obviously she was not unconquered in every aspect, for the tyrant not able to find what he sought yet found what he had not sought.

19.  How much stronger are our virgins who triumph over even the powers which they do not see. Their victory is not only over flesh and blood but also over the prince of the world and the ruler of this age! Agnes was the younger in age but the older in virtue, the greater of her triumph, the more dauntless her constancy. She did not destroy her tongue through fear, but preserved it as a trophy, for there was nothing that she feared to betray—she whose confession was not shameful but religious. And so whereas the former merely concealed her secret, the latter bore witness to God. Her nature confessed what her years did not allow her to confess.

20.  It is the custom in eulogies to speak of the country of birth and the parentage so that in bringing to mind the ancestral background, the dignity of the descendent may be enhanced. Granted

that I have not set out to praise virginity but rather to describe it, yet I think it pertinent to make known its native land and its parent. Now first let us determine where is the land of its origin. For if one's country is the place of one's birth, then really, heaven is the birthplace of chastity; here it is alien, but there native.

21. Now what is virginal chastity other than purity free from contagion? And whom can we consider to be its author other than the immaculate Son of God whose flesh saw no corruption and whose divinity was free from contagion? Therefore you see how great are the merits of virginity. Christ was before the virgin, Christ was of the virgin; from the Father before the ages, but born of the virgin for the ages. The former was of his own nature, but this is for our sake. That always was, this was what he willed.

22. Consider yet another merit of virginity; Christ is the spouse of the virgin, and, if one may say so, Christ is the spouse of virginal chastity. For virginity is of Christ, not Christ of virginity. Therefore it is a virgin who is espoused, a virgin who carries us in the womb, a virgin who gives birth, a virgin who nourishes with her own milk, of whom we read, "What great things has the virgin Jerusalem done! Neither from the rocks shall the breast dry up, not the snow from Lebanon, nor shall the water borne by the strong wind fail (cf. Jer. 18:13). What kind of a virgin is this who is watered by the fountains of the Trinity; for whom do the waters flow from the rock, breasts not fail, and honey is outpoured? Now, for the apostle, the rock is Christ (1 Cor. 10:14). Therefore from Christ the breasts do not fail, nor from God the brightness, nor from the Spirit the river. This is the Trinity which waters its church—the Father, Son, and Spirit.

23. But now from consideration of the mother, we come down to the daughters. "Concerning virgins," said the holy apostles, "I have no precept of the Lord" (1 Cor. 7:25). If the teacher of the Gentiles had none, who could possibly have one? And indeed he did not have a commandment, but he had an example. For virginity cannot be imposed but is opted for. For things that are beyond our nature are rather matters for prayer than for directive instruction. "But," he says, "I wish you to be free of concern. For he who is without a wife is concerned for the things of the Lord, how he may please God . . . and the virgin thinks of the things of the Lord, that she may be holy in body and spirit. For she who is married takes thought of the things of the world, how she may please her husband" (1 Cor. 7:32–34).

24. Indeed, I am not discouraging marriage but am enlarging upon the privilege of virginity. "He who is weak," says the apostle, "let him eat herbs." I reflect upon the one, I admire the other. "Are you bound to a wife? Do not seek to be freed. Are you free from a wife? Do not seek a wife" (1 Cor. 7:27). This commandment is for the married. But what does he have to say about virginity? "And he who gives his virgin in marriage does well, but he who does not give her does better" (1 Cor. 7:38). The former does not sin if she marries; the latter if she does not marry is turned toward eternity. On the one hand is the remedy for weakness, on the other, the glory of chastity. The first is not to be reproached, the second is to be praised.

25. Let us compare, if I may, the advantages of married women with the expectations of virgins. Granted that the noble woman may boast of her numerous offspring; but the greater number she bears, the more she endures. Let her count the solace of her children but let her count the vexations as well. She marries and she weeps. What kind of vows are those which are made in tears? She conceives and grows heavy. Her fruitfulness brings an encumbrance even before offspring. She gives birth and she is ill. How sweet the pledge which begins in danger and ends in danger, in which sorrow will have priority over pleasure! It is purchased by dangers but it is not acquired by virtue of free will.

26. Why should I dwell on the troubles of nursing, of training, and other aspects of married life. These are the miseries of the fortunate! A mother has heirs, but it increases her sorrows. On the other hand, one ought not to make reference to adversities lest the souls of the holiest parents tremble. See, my sister, how hard it must be to suffer what ought not be mentioned. And this in the present age! But the days will come when they will say, "Blessed are the barren, and the wombs which have not borne" (Luke 23:29). For the daughters of this age are conceived and conceive; but the daughter of the kingdom abstains from married pleasure, and carnal pleasure, so that she may be holy in body and spirit.

27. Why should I expound further on the heavy servitude and bounden duty of married women to their husbands, the service ordered by God before that of slaves (Gen. 3:16)? And I go on to mention these things only that they may obey in a better frame of mind; if they are virtuous, this is repaid with love, if lacking in virtue, it exacts a penalty.

28. It is from these circumstances that an incentive toward vice is born; they paint their faces with a range of colors while they fear to displease their husbands, yet from the falsifying of their countenance, they begin to consider the falsification of chastity. What madness this, to change the likeness of nature, to seek a painted representation, and while revering their husband's judgment, they betray him! For she is the first to witness against herself who wishes to change what is hers by birth, and so while she endeavors to please others, she first displeases herself. Woman, what more telling witness of your deformity do we require other than you yourself who fear to be seen! If you are beautiful, what do you hide? If ugly, why do you pretend to a loveliness that gives you neither the gratification that comes from your conscience nor a stranger's mistake? For he loves another—you wish to please another; and you will be angered if he loves another—he who is taught falsehood in your own person. You are an evil teacher resulting in your own injury. A woman avoids to entice for immoral purposes, and yet she has endured the enticer. And granted that she may not be an immoral woman, though she may not have sinned against another, yet she has sinned against herself. Almost every other crime is more tolerable—for these, chastity may be corrupted, but here it is nature itself that suffers.

29. Now what a costly enterprise it is so that even beauty may not be displeasing! And for this the precious chains are hung around the neck; for this, a golden robe is dragged along the ground. Is this beauty purchased or is it possessed? And what of the various perfumes used for enticement! The ears are weighed down with gems and the eyes are smeared with other colors. What is left when so much is changed? The woman lets go of her own senses and believes it possible to go on living!

30. But it is true that you, blessed virgins, who know nothing of the things that are torments rather than ornaments, you for whom the holy purity suffusing your modest face and lovely chastity are the adornment. You do not assent to the critique of human eyes—weighing your merit by another's mistake. You have indeed the service of your own beauty, to which the loveliness of virtue is in service, not that of the body. Age does not destroy it, death can take nothing away, nor can sickness spoil it. Let God alone be sought as the judge of loveliness—God who loves in less beautiful bodies, the more beautiful souls. You do not know the heaviness of the womb or the pain of childbearing.

Nevertheless, more numerous are the offspring of the pious mind which has all things as its children. Fruitful in progeny, barren in bereavement, knowing nothing of funerals, but knowing heirs.

31. And so, too, the holy church, immaculate in her union, fruitful in childbearing, is a virgin in her chastity and a mother in her offspring. Filled by the Spirit, not by a husband, as a virgin she gives birth to us. As a virgin she bears us, not with the pain of bodily members, but with the rejoicing of angels. As a virgin she nourishes us, not with bodily milk, but with that given by the apostle to a people who were as yet weak and still of a tender age (cf. 1 Cor. 3:2). What bride has more children than the holy church, who is a virgin in her sacraments, a mother in her people; to whose fruitfulness even Scripture attests, saying, "How many are the children of the desolate, more than she who has a husband" (Isa. 54:1). Our mother has not a husband, but she has a bridegroom. For whether as the church among the people or whether as the soul in the individual, without being violated by any deviation from modesty yet pregnant with wisdom, she weds the Word of God as her eternal spouse.

32. Parents, you have heard of the virtues and of the training you ought to inculcate in your daughters, so that you may have those who may redeem you through their merits. A virgin is the gift of God, the pledge for her parents—the priesthood of chastity. A virgin is the offering of her mother. By her daily sacrifice the divine power is appeased. A virgin is the undivided security of her parents; for she neither troubles them for a dowry nor forsakes them by going away nor displeases them by wrongdoing.

33. But someone may wish to have grandchildren and to be called a grandfather. So first, in seeking what belongs to another, he gives up what is his own. Next he begins to suffer the loss of what is his for certain, while he pins his hopes on what is an uncertainty. He gives away his own wealth, and yet still more is demanded. If he does not pay the dowry, it is exacted; if he is long-lived, he is a burden. This is what it is to purchase a son-in-law, one who would sell even a glimpse of their daughter to her parents! This can hardly be described as a gain. Was it for this that she was carried so many months in her mother's womb, just so she would pass under the power of another? Was it for this that the duty of the care of a virgin is undertaken—that she may be taken from her parents the more quickly?

34. But someone may say, Do you speak against marriage? I certainly encourage it and condemn those who are accustomed to argue against marriage. And as often as possible I am in the habit of holding up the marriage of Sarah, Rebecca, and Rachel and the other women of the past as instances of outstanding virtues. For he who condemns marriage, condemns children as well and condemns the human society continued through the series of successive generations. For how would it be possible for age to succeed age, generation after generation, unless the nuptial grace stirred up the desire for offspring? Or how is it possible to proclaim that an immaculate Isaac went forward to the altar of God as a victim of his father's piety (Gen. 21:2), or that, while still in the bodily condition, Israel saw God (Gen. 32:27) and gave a religious name to the people—how is it possible to proclaim the deeds and condemn the origin? In condemning marriage, these men, sacrilegious though they be, have at least one argument with which the wisest could concur—that they should never have been born!

35. Thus I am not discouraging marriage but expounding upon the fruits of holy virginity. This is the gift of only a few, the other is for all. Certainly virginity is not able to exist unless it has a mode of coming into being. I am comparing good to good to clarify which is more excellent; and I am not putting forward my own opinion, but I am repeating what the Holy Spirit made known through the prophet: "Better is childlessness with virtue" (Wisd. of Sol. 4:1).

36. First of all, while those who are able to marry desire above anything else to boast of the handsome appearance of their bridegroom, they must admit that here they are inferior to virgins who alone can rightly say, "You are more beautiful in appearance than the sons of men, grace is poured out on your lips" (Ps. 45:2). Who is this bridegroom? Not one given to low indulgence, but he whose throne is for all eternity. The daughters of the king stand within his honor. "The queen stands at your right hand in a robe of gold, invested with a variety"—of virtues. Therefore "listen, daughter, and see and incline your ear, and forget your people and your father's house, for the King has greatly desired your beauty, for he is your God" (Ps. 45:10–11).

37. And just think how much the Holy Spirit has offered you through the testimony of the divine Scriptures—a kingdom, gold, beauty: a kingdom, either because you are the bride of an eternal

king, or because carrying an unconquered mind, you have not been captivated by the allurements of pleasure, on the contrary, you rule like a queen; gold, because as that metal is more precious when it is tested by fire, so the beauty of the virginal body, consecrated by the Holy Spirit, requires an increase in its own loveliness; beauty, indeed, for who can appraise the loveliness of her who is loved by the King, approved by the Judge, dedicated to the Lord and consecrated to God—ever espoused, ever unmarried, so that neither love comes to an end, nor modesty suffers harm.

38. This is indeed true beauty, to which nothing is wanting, and which alone merits to hear from the Lord, "You are all beautiful, my dearest, and in you there is no blemish. My Spouse, come from Lebanon, come from Lebanon, you shall pass and pass through from the beginning of faith, from the top of Samir and Hermon, from the dens of lions, from the mountains of leopards" (Song of Sol. 4:7, 8 LXX). By these references is shown the perfect and irreprehensible beauty of virginal souls, consecrated at the divine altars—souls among the haunts and the dens of spiritual beasts, unmoved by things mortal, but intent, through the mysteries of God, to be deserving of the Beloved, whose breasts are full of joy for "wine gladdens the human heart" (Ps. 104:15).

39. "The perfume," he says, "of your garments is beyond all spices," and continues, "the perfume of your garments is like the scent of Lebanon" (Song of Sol. 4:10, 11). See what a course is assigned to you, virgin. For your first perfume, "beyond all spices," which were used for the burial of the Lord, shows by its fragrance that the motions of the body are dead, meaning that the pleasures of its members have died. Your second perfume exhales the incorruption of the Lord's body, the flower of virginal chastity.

40. Let your works form as it were a honeycomb of sweetness, for virginity deserves to be compared to bees, being so industrious, so modest, so self-controlled. The bee feeds on dew, it knows no marriage bed, it forms honey. The dew of the virgin is the divine utterance—because the words of God descend like dew. The modesty of the virgin is of an unstained nature. The dew of the virgin is the fruit of the lips, without bitterness, overflowing with sweetness. The labor is in common, the fruit is for the common good.

41. Daughter, how I wish you to be an imitator of this little bee whose food is the flower, whose offspring is gathered by mouth

and formed by mouth. Imitate it, daughter. Let no veil of deceit be spread over your words, let there be no fraudulent covering over them so that they may be pure and dignified.

42. From your mouth, may an everlasting progeny of merits be born to you. But not for yourself alone, but for the many (for how do you know when your soul will be required of you?) lest leaving the granaries heaped up with grain advantageous neither to your life nor your merits, you be hurried away where you cannot bring your treasure. Therefore be rich, but rich for the poor, that as they share your nature, may they also share your wealth.

43. And I also point out the flower which is to be culled. Assuredly it is the one who said, "I am the flower of the field and the lily of the valley; I am as a lily among thorns" (Song of Sol. 2:12). This is a clear indication that virtues are beset by thorns of spiritual evil, and no one may gather the fruit who does not approach with caution.

44. Virgin, take wings, but wings of the Spirit, so that you may soar above the vices if you desire to reach Christ. "He dwells on high and looks upon the lowly" (Ps. 113:5). And his appearance is that of a cedar of Lebanon whose foliage is in the clouds while its roots are set in the earth. For its beginning is from heaven, its ending is on earth, and it produces its fruit nearest heaven. Search all the more diligently for so excellent a flower. It may well be that you find it somewhere in the valley of your heart, for frequently its perfume breathes upon the lowly.

45. This flower loves to grow in gardens where Suzanna discovered it as she was walking, and she was prepared to die rather than have it violated (cf. Dan. 13:7). But he himself shows what is meant by the garden when he says, "A garden enclosed, a fountain sealed" (Song of Sol. 4:12). Because it is there in such gardens that the water of the pure fountains impressed by the seals is made resplendent by the image of God lest its streams muddied from the wallowing of spiritual wild beasts be polluted. So just as a garden inaccessible to thieves is redolent of the vine, has the ardor of the olive, and is resplendent with the rose, so may religion flourish in the vine, peace in the olive, and the modesty of consecrated virginity in the rose. This is the perfume with which the patriarch Jacob was enthralled when he merited to hear, "Behold, the smell of my son is like the smell of an abundant field." For granted that the field of the holy patriarch was full of almost all fruits, yet the one with greater labor produced the fruits of virtue, the other flowers.

46. So forearm yourself, virgin, and if you wish your garden to be sweet like this, fence it in with the precepts of the prophets. "Place a guard before your mouth, and a door to your lips" (Ps. 141:3), for then you will be able to say, "As an apple tree among the trees of the woods, so is my brother among the sons. In his shadow I delighted and sat down, and his fruit was sweet to my palate. . . . I found him whom my soul loved, I held him and would not let him go . . . my brother came down into his garden to eat the fruit of his apple trees . . . my brother, let us go into the field. . . . Place me as a signet upon your heart and as a seal upon your arm . . . my brother is white and ruddy" (Song of Sol. 2:3; 3:4; 5:1; 7:11; 8:6; 5:10). For it is only fitting, virgin, that you should have complete knowledge of the one you love and recognize in him the whole mystery both of the unborn divinity and of the assumption of the bodily condition. Appropriately he is white, because he is the splendor of the Father—ruddy, because he is born of a virgin. In him the color of both natures is glowing and radiant. Remember, however, that in him the distinguishing marks of his divinity are much older than the sacraments of the body; for he did not begin existence from a virgin, but he who was came into a virgin.

47. He, who was torn by the soldiers, who was wounded by the lance (John 19:34) that he might heal us by the bloodiness of his sacred wounds, will surely answer you (for he is meek and humble of heart and gentle of aspect), "Arise, north wind, come, south wind, blow upon my garden and let my perfume flow out" (Song of Sol. 4:16). For from all parts of the world the scent of consecrated religion has increased and the members of the beloved virgin have become radiant. "You are lovely, my dearest, as good repute has it, beautiful as Jerusalem" (Song of Sol. 6:4). The loveliness of virgins is not the beauty of the fallen body, which can be destroyed by sickness or old age, but the reputation for merits which are subject to no decay.

48. And since you are already able to be compared not with human but with celestial beings whose life you live on earth, receive from the Lord the precept which you are to observe: "Place me as a signet," he says, "on your heart and as a seal upon your arm" (Song of Sol. 8:6). By this may be shown clearer proofs of your prudence and of your works in which Christ, the form of God, may shine—who being equal in all respects to the nature of the Father gave expression to the totality of the divinity he assumed from the Father. So also the apostle Paul says that we are

sealed in the Spirit (cf. Eph. 1:13) for in the Spirit we have the image of the Father, in the Spirit we have the signet of the Son. Sealed by the Spirit let us be more diligent lest by levity of conduct or any deceit of infidelity we break the seal of the pledge which we received in our hearts.

49.  But let fear secure this for the holy virgins for whom the church first provided such protection. Anxious for the well-being of her tender offspring, she—a strong wall with abundant breasts like towers—increases her care for them, until as the fear of hostile attack is ended she obtains peace for her vigorous young ones by the protection of her maternal strength. So it was the prophet said, "Let there be peace in your strength and abundance in your towers" (Ps. 122:7).

50.  Then the Lord of peace himself after he had embraced with his strong arms the vineyards committed to him and had seen the young vines beginning to shoot, tempers the breezes for the young fruits with watchful gaze as he himself testifies, "My vineyard is in my sight, a thousand for Solomon and two hundred who guard its fruits" (Song of Sol. 8:12).

51.  Before that he said, "Sixty men of might surround his offspring, armed with drawn swords and trained in military discipline" (Song of Sol. 3:7–8); now there are a thousand and two hundred—the number increasing where the fruit increases, for the holier one is, the more one is guarded. So it was that Elishah the prophet demonstrated that an army of angels was present to guard him (Josh. 5:14; 2 Kings 6:17); so it was that Joshua, son of Nun, recognized the captain of the heavenly army. It is sure that they who can fight for us are well able to guard the fruit in us. But for you, holy virgins, there is a special protection, you who with unstained purity keep holy the marriage bed of the Lord. It is hardly to be wondered if the angels war for you who yourself do battle in an angelic mode. Virginal chastity deserves the protection of those whose way of life it deserves.

52.  And why spend any further words in praising chastity? For chastity has made angels. The one who kept it is an angel, the one who lost it is a devil. In this way even religion has acquired a name. A virgin is one who espouses God, a harlot one who makes gods. Now what shall I say about the resurrection—whose rewards you already lay hold of? "In the resurrection they will neither marry, nor be given in marriage, but they will be," he says, "as the angels in heaven" (Matt. 22:30). What is promised to us is,

for you, a present reality and the benefits accruing from our prayers are already with you. You are of this world and yet are not in this world. This age has merited to have you, yet cannot retain you.

53. How extraordinary that angels, because of lack of discipline fell from heaven into this world, while virgins, through chastity, pass from this world into heaven! Blessed virgins, whom the delights of the body do not allure nor the flood of pleasures sweep away! Fasts from food and abstinence from drink teach ignorance of the causes of the vices, for that which causes sin has often deceived even the just. In this way, the people of God, after sitting down to eat and drink, denied God (Exod. 32:6). In this way, Lot was unaware that he was lying with his daughters, and so endured it (Gen. 19:33). In this way, stepping backward, the sons of Noah covered up with garments their father's nakedness; the shameless one looked, the modest son blushed, the filial son covered him, fearing to offend if he himself looked (Gen. 9:22). What strength is in wine—he whom the flood could not denude was made nude by wine!

54. A further point! What a deep happiness it is that no desire for possessions inflames you! The poor ask for what you have, they do not demand what you do not have. The fruit of your labor is a treasure for the needy, and two small coins—if that is all there is—are riches on the part of the liberal giver. Listen, sister, how much you escape from. But it is not for me to teach or for you to learn what you should be cautious about; for the practice of perfect virtue has no wish for instructions, but rather it educates. You see that she who sets out to please, displaying herself like the litters in the festivities, turning all heads and gazes towards her, is all the more ugly in herself because she sets out to please—first because she displeased the people rather than pleased her husband. But in you the disdain for beauty preparations is more fitting, and the fact that you do not adorn yourself is in itself an adornment.

55. Look at the ears lacerated with wounds, and pity the neck weighed down with loads. The difference in metal does not lighten the suffering. Here a chain binds the neck, there a shackle encloses the foot; it makes no difference whether the body is loaded with gold or with iron—here the neck is weighed down, there the steps are hindered. The cost is of no advantage unless it is, women, that you fear to lose what punishes you! What does it

matter whether it is the sentence of someone else or your own that condemns you? You are surely more pitiable than people condemned by a public court since they desire to be freed—you to be bound!

56. How truly pitiful is it that the girl of marriageable age is bid for money as if it were a form of slavery. In fact the selling of slaves is, in a sense, more tolerable because they often choose their masters whereas, if a virgin chooses, it is a crime, if she does not choose it is an affront. However beautiful and attractive she may be, she fears and, at the same time, desire to be seen. She desires to be seen to sell herself at the highest price; she fears to be seen lest that in itself is unbecoming. What a deal of absurdity in the form of fervent wishes, of fears and suspicions as to how the suitors will turn out—lest an impoverished man practice deception, lest a rich man be fastidious, lest a handsome suitor ridicule, lest a nobleman spurn her!

57. Someone may complain—you sing the praises of virginity to us every day. But what do I accomplish who sing of it daily to no avail? But do not blame me. In the end, virgins come from Placentia, they come from Bononia, they come from Mauritania to receive the veil here. You see how extraordinary! Here, I treat of the matter; there, I persuade. If this is the result, I should hold my discourse elsewhere so that I may persuade you.

58. Why is it, then, that those who do not hear my words, follow my teaching while those who hear do not? For I have known many virgins who had the intention of coming forward but were prevented by their mothers—and, what is more serious, by the widows to whom I here address myself. To be sure, if your daughters wished to love a man, by law they could choose whomever they wished. Are they who are permitted to choose a man, not allowed to choose God?

59. Consider how sweet is the fruit of modesty which has grown even in the affections of barbarians! From the most distant territories either side of Mauritania, virgins are eager to come here to be consecrated; and while the families are in captivity, yet modesty does not know what it is to be held captive. She who grieves over the injustice of slavery avows an eternal kingdom.

60. And what shall I say about the virgins of Bononia, a fertile band of modesty who themselves renouncing the delight of this world, live in a holy shrine of virginity? Without companionship of the opposite sex, through their companionship in modesty

they have increased twentyfold in number, and a hundredfold in fruit; they have left the love of their parents, and as soldiers of unwearied chastity they press on to the tabernacles of Christ. At one time exulting with spiritual canticles, at another earning their livelihood through work, they seek with their hands the provision for their liberality.

61. If the scent grows strong in this search for virgins (for above all others they are to the fore in the chase after modesty) they pursue their hidden prey to their very chambers with every mark of solicitude; or if anyone's flight glitters more liberally, you may see all rise up together, flap their feathers, and soar into gleaming flight with loud applause so that they may encircle with a chaste chorus of modesty the one taking flight; and so at length, rejoicing in that lovely companionship, forgetful of her father's house, she enters the domains of modesty and the enclosure of chastity.

62. It is certainly a good thing if the zeal of the parents, like favoring winds of modesty, should aid the virgin; but it is even more glorious if without the nurturing of her elders, the fire of tender youth should spontaneously ignite the tinder of chastity. Parents will refuse a dowry, but you have a rich spouse. Satisfied with his treasures, you will not strive for the profits of a paternal inheritance. How much does chaste poverty surpass the wealth accruing from dowries!

63. And have you ever heard of anyone's being deprived of her lawful inheritance because of her zeal for integrity of life? Parents speak out against her intention, but they want to be won over. First they resist because they fear to believe; very often they are indignant so that you may learn to get the better of them. They threaten to disinherit to find out if you can be unafraid of the loss of the goods of this world. They coax with delicate allurements to see whether the blandishments of various pleasures may not soften you. You are being exercised, virgin, while you are enduring constraint; and the anxious entreaties put forward by your parents are your battle. Young woman, first conquer filial affection. First you conquer your home, then you conquer the world.

64. But suppose the loss of your patrimony awaits you, should not the future kingdom of heaven compensate for the losses of unstable and perishable wealth? Should we not give credence to the heavenly words "There is no one who has forsaken home, or parents, or brother or wives or sons for the sake of the kingdom

of God who will not receive seven times as much in this life and in the world to come will possess eternal life" (cf. Matt. 19:29–30)? Entrust your faith to God; you who entrust your money to men, lend to Christ. The faithful custodian of your deposit of hope repays your faith investment with multiple interest. For truth does not cheat, justice does not defraud, virtue cannot deceive. If you do not believe the inspired utterances, at least believe examples.

65. I remember a girl at one time noble in this world, now more noble in the sight of God who, when she was being urged to matrimony by her parents and relatives, took refuge at the consecrated altar. What better place for a virgin than where the sacrifice of virginity is offered! Nor was that the limit of her daring. She stood at the altar of God as a sacrifice of modesty, as a victim of chastity, now placing the right hand of the priest upon her head and asking for prayers, now impatient at the just delay, bowing under the altar. "Can there be any more fitting veil for me than the altar which sanctifies the veils themselves? What more becoming than the bridal veil on which Christ, the head of all, is daily consecrated? What are you doing, my relatives? Why do you still trouble my mind with seeking after marriage? I have long since provided for that. You offer me a bridegroom? I have found a better. Exaggerate wealth as much as you like, talk about nobility, boast of power—I possess him to whom no one can be compared: rich in the world, powerful in empire, noble in heaven. If you promote such a person, I do not reject your choice; if you do not find such a one, you are not provident towards me, my parents, but do me an injury." While the rest were reduced to silence, one spoke out abruptly. "If your father were alive would he have allowed you to remain unmarried?" She, then, with deeper religious conviction and more restrained piety, responded, "Perhaps it was for that reason that he has departed so that no one could present a hindrance." And that this response concerning her father was really an oracle about himself was proved by his own sudden death. So the rest of them, each one fearing for himself, began to assist when they had previously sought to discourage her. Her virginity did not result in the loss of the property to which she was entitled, but also received the reward of integrity. Young girls, you see the reward of devotion. Parents be warned by the example of obstruction.

# VIII.

## Augustine of Hippo

### ON THE FIRST EPISTLE OF JOHN,
### SERMON X

1. I trust you recall, those of you who were here yesterday, how far we had reached in our homily in the course of this epistle: "For he who does not love the brother whom he sees, how can he love the God whom he does not see?" And we have this commandment from him, "That he who loves God loves his brother also" (1 John 4:20–21). This has been discussed, now let us see what comes next in order.

"Whoever believes that Jesus is the Christ, is born of God" (1 John 5:1). Who is the one who does not believe that Jesus is the Christ? The one who does not live as Christ commands. For many say, "I believe," but faith without works does not save. For the work of faith is love itself, as the apostle Paul says, ". . . and faith which works through love" (Gal. 5:6). For in fact your previous works before you became to believe were either nonexistent or, if they appeared to be good, were worthless. If they were nonexistent then you were either as a man without feet or with sore feet not sound enough for walking; if, however, they appeared to be good, before you came to believe, then indeed you were running, but by running the wrong way you were going farther astray instead of reaching the finishing line. It is for us then both to run and to run along the right way. He who runs along the wrong way, runs in vain, or rather, he runs only for the labor. The more he goes astray, the farther he runs the wrong way. What is the only way along which we should run? Christ said, "I am the Way." To which home country do we run? Christ said, "I am the Truth." By him you run, to him you run, in him you are at rest. But so that it is by him that we run, he reaches out to us—we were far astray and were travelling in distant countries. It was bad enough that we were so far distant but in our weakened state we could barely move. A Physician came to the sick, a Way was extended to the travellers. By him, let us be saved, through him, let us walk.

This is what it means to believe that Jesus is the Christ, as Christians believe; who are not just Christians by name but by deeds and by lifestyle: it is not as the demons believe. For "the demons believe and tremble" (James 2:19) says Scripture. For what more could the demons believe than to say "we know who you are, the Son of God" (cf. Matt. 8:29; Mark 1:24)? What the demons said, Peter said the selfsame thing. When the Lord asked them who he was, and whom men said he was, the disciples responded, "Some say you are John the Baptist, others Elias, others Jeremias or one of the Prophets" (Matt. 16:14). And to Peter, "But, you, who do you say that I am?" and he answered, "You are the Christ, the Son of the living God"; and he heard from the Lord, "Blessed are you, Simon Bar Jonah; because flesh and blood has not revealed it to you, but my Father who is in heaven" (Matt. 16:15–17). See what praise follows this faith. "You are Peter and upon this rock I will build my church" (Matt. 16:18). What does it mean, "Upon this rock I will build my church"? Upon this faith, upon this statement, "You are the Christ, the Son of the living God." "Upon this rock," he said, "I will lay the foundation of my church." What great praise! So Peter says, "You are the Christ, the Son of the living God"; the demons say, "We know who you are, the Son of God, the Holy One of God" (Mark 1:24)? Peter says this, and the demons also say this, the same words, but not the same intent! And how can it be established that Peter spoke these words out of love? For a Christian's faith is expressed with love, whereas a demon's is devoid of love. How is it loveless? Peter said this that he might draw near to Christ, the demons said this that Christ might draw away from them. Because before they said, "We know who you are; you are the Son of God," they said, "What is there in common between you and us? Why have you come to destroy us before the time?" For it is one thing to confess Christ that you may cling to Christ; it is quite another to confess Christ that you may drive Christ away from you.

So you see what is meant when he says here, "Whoever believes"; that it is one's own faith, not what is held in common with a crowd. Therefore, brothers, do not let the heretics say to you—"we, too, believe." For I have put before you the example of the demons, so that you may not find joy in words of belief, but search out the deeds of life.

2. We have seen, then, what it is to believe in Christ; it is to believe that Jesus himself is the Christ. The text continues, "Whoever believes that Jesus is the Christ is born of God" (1 John 5:1). But what does it mean to believe that? "And everyone who loves the one who begot him, also loves him who was begotten of such a One." Immediately he conjoins love with faith, because without love, faith is in vain. Conjoined with love, it is the faith of a Christian; devoid of love it is the faith of a demon. But those who do not believe are worse than demons, and more stupid than demons. I do not know how it is that someone would not wish to believe in Christ. At this point, one does not even imitate the demons. Now a person believes in Christ, but hates Christ; the confession of faith stems from fear of punishment, but not from love of the crown; thus the demons also feared to be punished. Add love to this faith, so that it may become the kind of faith of which the apostle Paul speaks, "faith which works through love" (Gal. 5:6), and you have found a Christian, you have found a citizen of Jerusalem, you have found a fellow citizen of the angels, you have a pilgrim sighing along the way. Go to join him, he is your companion, run with him, if you, too, are such a one: "Whoever loves the one who begot him, also loves him who was begotten of such a one." Who begot? The Father. Who was begotten? The Son. Therefore what does he say? "Whoever loves the Father, loves the Son."

3. "In this we know that we love the sons of God" (1 John 5:2). What is this, brothers? A little before he was speaking of the Son of God, not of the sons of God; see how one Christ was placed before us for contemplation, and it was said to us, "Whoever believes that Jesus is the Christ, is born of God, and everyone who loves is born of him"—that is, the Father, "loves him who was begotten of him", that is the Son, our Lord Jesus Christ. And he goes on, "In this we know that we love the sons of God"—just as if he were about to say, "In this we know that we love the Son of God." He said "sons of God" when a little before he was saying "Son of God," because the sons of God are the body of the only Son of God; and since he is the head, and we are the members, there is but one Son of God. Therefore whoever loves the sons of

God loves the Son of God, and whoever loves the Son of God loves the Father; nor can anyone love the Father without loving the Son, and whoever loves the Son, loves the sons of God.

What sons of God? The members of the Son of God. It is through loving that one becomes oneself a member, and through love, one becomes part of the structure of the body of Christ; and there will be but one Christ loving himself. For when the members love one another, the body loves itself. "And if one member suffers, all the members suffer with it, and if one member is glorified, all the members rejoice together" (1 Cor. 12:26, 27). And what does John go on to say after this? "But now you are the body of Christ and members." Speaking a little before about brotherly love, he said, "Whoever does not love the brother he sees, how can he love God whom he does not see? (1 John 4:20). But if you love the brother, perhaps it may be that you love the brother, and do not love Christ? How could this be, when you love the members of Christ? For when you love the members of Christ, you love Christ; when you love Christ, you love the Son of God; when you love the Son of God, you love the Father. Therefore it is impossible to divide love. Choose what you will love, the rest will follow you. You may say, I love God alone, God the Father. You lie. If you love, you do not love him alone; but if you love the Father, you also love the Son. Look, you say, I love the Father and I love the Son—but only these—God the Father and God the Son, Our Lord Jesus Christ who ascended the heavens and sits at the right hand of the Father, that Word through whom all things were made and "the Word was made flesh and dwelt among us" (John 1:14). This only do I love. You lie. For if you love the Head, you love the members also. But if you do not love the members neither do you love the Head. Do you not feel terror at the voice of the Head crying out from heaven on behalf of his members, "Saul, Saul, why do you persecute me?" (Acts 9:4). He called the persecutor of his members, his persecutor; he calls the lover of his members, his lover. Now you know who are his members, brothers. It is none other than the church of God. "In this we know that we love the sons of God, because we love God" (1 John 5:2). But how? Are not the sons of God one thing, but God himself another? But whoever loves God, loves his precepts. And what are the precepts of God? "A new commandment I give to you, that you love one another" (John 13:34). Let no one excuse himself from one love by virtue of another. This love of yours must be utterly coherent; it has itself been bonded together into a unity in such a way that everything depends upon it, and makes a single whole as if fused together by fire. It is gold; the mass is melted down and become one. But unless the warmth of charity kindles it from above, it is not possible that out of many can there be a melting into one. "Because we love God, then we know that we love the sons of God."

4. And how do we know that we love the sons of God? Because we love God, and do his commandments (1 John 5:2). Here we sigh because of the difficulty of doing the commands of God. But listen to what follows. What do you labor to love? Avarice. With strain is loved what you love: There is no strain in loving God. Avarice imposes hardships, dangers, torments, and tribulations, and you will submit to this. To what end? To acquire that which may fill a money chest and cost your peace of mind. Perhaps you were more secure before you had possessions than after. See what avarice demands of you. You have stocked up your house, and thieves are feared. You acquire gold and lose sleep. See what avarice demands of you. Do this and you do it! What does God demand of you?—Love me. You love gold, you will be in search of gold, and it may not be found; God promises, whoever seeks me, I am with him. You will love honor, and perhaps you will not attain it: God says, who has loved me, and not attained to me? God says to you You wish to make for yourself a protector, or a powerful friend; you court him through another inferior. Love me, God says to you; the way to win my favor is not through someone else. Your love itself makes me present to you. What is sweeter than this love, brothers? It is not without reason that you have just heard in the Psalm, "The unjust told me of their delights, but it is not as your Law, Oh Lord" (cf. Ps. 119:85). What is the Law of God? The commandment of God. What is the commandment of God? It is that new commandment which is said to be "new" because it renews. "A new commandment I give to you, that you love one another" (John 13:34). Listen because this is indeed the Law of God. The Apostle says, "Bear one another's burdens, and so you will fulfill the law of Christ" (Gal. 6:2). It is this that is the consummation of all our works—love. There is the goal; for this we run; when we will come to this we shall rest.

5. You have heard in the Psalms, "I have seen the end of all perfection" (Ps. 119:96). He said, "I have seen the end of all perfection." What is it that he had seen? Do we think that he had

climbed up to the peak of some high and precipitous mountain
and from that perspective had gazed upon the outer boundaries
of the earth and the circles of the universe; and that is why he said
"I have seen the end of all perfection?" If this is what is praised
then let us ask the Lord for bodily eyes so keen-sighted that we
only need some extremely high mountain from whose summit
we may see the end of all perfection. Do not go so far: Look I tell
you, ascend the mountain and see the end. Christ is the mountain, come to Christ; from there you see the end of all perfection.
What is this end? Ask Paul: "But the end of the commandment is
the charity of a pure heart, a good conscience, and a sincere
faith" (1 Tim. 1:5). And elsewhere he says, "But charity is the
fulfillment of the law" (Rom. 13:10). What is more "ended" and
"terminated" than fulfillment? Indeed, brothers, he poses the
word "end" as praiseworthy. Do not think in terms of consump-
tion, but consummation. For in one sense it is said, "I have finished the bread," in another, "I have finished the coat." I have
finished the bread by consuming it; I have finished the coat by
sewing it. And in each case the word "finish" is used. But the
bread is finished so that it will no longer exist, while the coat is
finished so that it will be perfect. You are to hear "end" in this
latter sense. When the Psalm is read you hear, "On the end, a
Psalm of David." You are constantly hearing this in the Psalms,
and you should understand what you hear. What is "on the end"?
"For Christ is the end of the law. He is the justification of all who
believe" (Rom. 10:4). And what does it mean, "Christ is the
end"? That Christ is God, and "the end of the commandment is
charity," and "God is charity," because Father, Son, and Holy
Spirit are one. There he is the end for you, elsewhere he is the
way. Do not go loitering along the way and so not arrive at the
end. Whatever else you come to, keep going until you arrive at the
end. What is the end? "For me it is good to hold fast to God" (Ps.
73:28). Hold fast to God, you have finished the way, you will
reside in your own country. Attend carefully! Someone seeks
after money; for you let it not be an end, but pass on like a traveller. Seek where to pass on, not where to stay behind. But, if you
love it you are entangled by avarice—for you, avarice will be as
shackles making further progress impossible. Pass by this, too;
seek the end. You seek health of body; still do not stop there. For
what is this health of body that is destroyed by death and that is
debilitated by sickness? Something trifling, mortal, and fleeting.

Certainly, seek it lest perhaps ill health impede your good works. But you can be sure that the end is not here because it is the means for something else, for whatever is sought for something else, there is not the end. Whatever is sought freely for its own sake; there is an end. You seek for honors; perhaps you seek to do something, to accomplish something to please God. Do not love the honor itself, lest you stop there. Do you seek praise? If you seek God's, you do well, but if you seek your own, you act badly. You are loitering along the way. But look, you are loved, you are praised! Do not congratulate yourself when you are praised for your own sake; be praised in the Lord that you may sing, "In the Lord my soul will be praised" (Ps. 34:2). You make some fine speech and it is admired? Do not accept the praise as your own, the end is not there. But if you make this the finish, you will be finished; but you will not be finished as made perfect, but finished as consumed. For this reason your speech is not to be praised as from you or as your own. But how is it to be praised? It says how in the psalm, "In God I shall praise speech, and in God I shall praise word" (cf. Ps. 56:10). May what follows be accomplished in you, "In God, I have hoped, I shall not fear what man may do to me" (Ps. 56:11). For when everything that is yours is praised in God there is no fear that your praise be lost because God does not fail. Pass on beyond this too.

6. You see, brothers, how much we are passing, and in what things, the end is not to be found. We use these things as means when we are on the way, as we refresh ourselves at rest stations, and pass on. Therefore where is the end? "Beloved, we are the sons of God, and what we will be is not yet apparent," here it is said in this epistle (1 John 3:2). And so till now we are on the way, till now wherever we come, we must pass on until we arrive at some end. "We know that when he will appear, we shall be like him because then we shall see him as he truly is" (1 John 3:2). This is indeed the end. There is the perpetual praising; there is endless alleluia which never fails.

Therefore this is the end he spoke of in the psalm, "I have seen the end of all perfection" (Ps. 119:96). And as though it were said to him, what is the end which you saw? "Your extremely broad commandment." This is the end, the breadth of the commandment. Charity is the breadth of the commandment, because where there is charity, there is no narrow. This is the breadth of which the apostle spoke when he said, "Our mouth is open to you, Corinthians; our heart is open wide, there is no narrowness in us" (2 Cor. 6:11, 12). Therefore, indeed is "your commandment extremely broad." What is the broad commandment? "A new commandment I give to you, that you love one another." Therefore charity is not narrow. Would you wish not to be "narrow" on the earth? Live in a broad expanse. For whatever anyone does to you, shall not make you narrow, because you love that which another cannot hurt: you love God, you love the brotherhood, you love the law, you love the church of God; it shall endure forever. You labor on earth, but you will attain the joy that is promised. Who can take from you what you love? If no one can take from you what you love, you sleep secure. Or, better, you watch carefully unless you lose in sleeping that which you love. For not without design was it said, "Give light to my eyes, lest I sleep in death" (Ps. 13:3). They who shut their eyes against charity, fall asleep in the concupiscence of carnal pleasure. Be vigilant, then. For these are pleasures—to eat, to drink, to indulge in excesses, to play, to hunt; all evils are consequent on these empty displays. Do we not know that these are pleasures? Who would deny that these give pleasure? But the law of God is more loved. Cry out against such enticements. "The unjust have spoken to me of delights, but such is not your law, O Lord" (Ps. 119:85). This delight endures. It endures not only as that to which you come, but also as that which calls you back when you run away.

7. "For this is the love of God, that we keep his precepts" (1 John 5:3). Now you have heard, "On these two precepts depend the whole of the law and the prophets" (Matt. 22:40). How does he prevent your attention being divided over a great many books? "On these two precepts depend the whole law and the prophets." On which two precepts? "You shall love the Lord your God with your whole heart, and your whole soul, and your whole mind," and "You shall love your neighbor as yourself. On these two precepts depend the whole law and the prophets." See to what precepts this whole epistle refers. Hold fast to love and you are fully secure. Do you fear to do harm to someone? Whom could you harm if you love them? Love, and it is not possible to do anything but good.

But perhaps you reproach someone. Tenderness does this, not harshness. Perhaps you strike? You do this for the sake of discipline. For the very tenderness of love does not allow you to abandon the undisciplined. And it can happen somehow that there are different and contrary results, in that sometimes hatred uses blandishment, while charity is harsh. Perhaps someone hates his enemy and pretends to a friendliness toward him. He sees him doing something evil and he praises him. He wishes him to fall headlong; he wishes him to plunge blindly over the steep incline of his unruly desires, and from there perhaps not to return. He praises "because the sinner is praised for the desires of his soul" (Ps. 10:3). He applies to him the unction of his adulation; so he hates, and he praises. Another sees his friend doing something of the kind, and he calls him back. If he does not listen he uses even scolding words; he rebukes, he quarrels. Sometimes it even comes to the point where then he must quarrels! See hatred offers blandishment and charity quarrels! Do not attend either to the words of blandishment or to the seeming harshness suffered in reproach. Look carefully at the vein, seek the root from which they proceed. The one offers blandishment to deceive, the other quarrels to correct.

It is not for us, brethren, to make you open wide your hearts; seek from God that you may love one another. Love all men, even your enemies, not because they are brothers but that they may be brothers—that you may always glow with fraternal love whether toward him who has already become a brother or to him who is an enemy, so that by being loved he may become a brother. Whenever you love a brother, you love a friend. From now on he is with you, now he is joined together with you in a unity that is truly catholic. If you are leading a good life, you love a brother transformed from an enemy. But if you love someone who at the present time does not believe in Christ, or if he believes in Christ, believes as the demons believe, you reprehend this falsity of his. But for your part, love, and love with brotherly tenderness. He is not yet a brother, but you love so that he may be a brother. Therefore the whole of our love is fraternal, toward Christians, toward all his members. The rule of charity, my brothers, its vigor, its flowers, fruit, beauty, charm, its food, drink, nourishment, and its embrace is without satiety. If it is thus that we delight as travelers, what shall be our rejoicing in our own country!

8. Let us run, then, my brothers, let us run and love Christ. Which Christ? Jesus Christ. Who is he? The Word of God. In what way did he come to the sick? "The Word was made flesh and made his dwelling among us" (John 1:14). Therefore what the

Scripture predicted is fulfilled, "Christ must suffer and rise again from the dead on the third day" (Luke 24:26). Where is his body to be found? Where do his members labor? Where should you be so that you may be under the head? "In his name, penance and remission of sins is to be preached to all the nations, beginning in Jerusalem" (Luke 24:47). There let your charity be spread abroad, Christ says this as does the Psalm, that is, the Spirit of God, "your commandment is broad," and yet someone may place limits to charity in Africa! Extend charity to the whole world, if you wish to love Christ, because the members of Christ are found throughout the world. If you love only a part, you are divided; if you are divided you are not in the body; if you are not in the body, you are not under the head.

What benefit is it when you believe and blaspheme at the same time? You adore him in the head, and blaspheme him in the body. He loves his body. If you cut yourself off from the body itself, the head had not cut itself off from the body. "You honor me without purpose," shouts the head to you from above. It is just as if someone wished to kiss you on the head and to trample on your feet. Perhaps he might pound your feet with hobnailed boots while wishing to clasp and kiss your head. Would you not cry out in the middle of these declarations of honor and say, "What are you doing, man? You are trampling on me." You do not say, "You are trampling on my head," because the head is being honored, but the head cries out all the more for the trampled members than for itself, which was being honored. Does not the head itself cry out, "I will have none of your honor, do not trample me"? Now you say, if you can, "How have I trampled on you?" Say this to the head, "I wished to kiss you, to embrace you." But do you not see, you foolish person, that, through a certain unity of bodily structure, what you wish to embrace reaches down to what you are trampling? Above, you honor me; below, you trample on me. What you trample upon feels more pain than what you honor feels glad, because what you honor suffers on behalf of what you trample. Why does the tongue cry out, "It hurts me"? It does not say, "It hurts my feet," but "It hurts me." O tongue, who has touched you? Who has struck? Who has tormented? Who has pierced? "No one—but I am joined to what is being trampled. How do you wish that I not feel pain, when I am not separated?"

9. Therefore our Lord Jesus Christ ascending to heaven on the fortieth day, entrusted to us his body which continued to lie here,

because he saw that he would be honored by many for having ascended to heaven. He also saw that if they trample his members on earth, the honor they offer is useless. And lest anyone should err and while adoring the head in heaven, trample the feet on earth, he said where his own members would be. For just as he was about to ascend he spoke his last words; after those very words he said nothing more on earth. The head who was about to ascend to heaven entrusted to us his members on earth and departed. From this time you do not find Christ speaking on earth; you find him speaking, but from heaven. And why from the heavens themselves? Because his members on earth are being trampled. For to Saul, the persecutor, he spoke from on high, "Saul, Saul, why do you persecute me?" I have ascended to heaven, but I still am to be found on earth; here I sit at the right hand of the Father, there still I hunger, I thirst, I am a traveller. In what way then did he entrust his body on earth when he was about to ascend? When his disciples asked him, "Will you present yourself at this time, and when will the kingdom of Israel be?" (Acts 1:6). And he replied just as he was about to leave, "It is not for you to know the time which the Father fixed by his own authority, but you are to receive the power of the Holy Spirit who will come upon you and you will be my witnesses" (Acts 1:7). See how the body is scattered abroad, see where he wishes it not to be trampled upon: "You will be my witnesses in Jerusalem, and in the whole of Judea, in Samaria and throughout the whole earth" (Acts 1:6–8). You see where I lie—I who ascend! For I ascend because I am the head. But still my body lies here. Where does it lie? Through all the earth. Take care lest you persecute, take care lest you do violence, take care lest you trample down." These are the last words of Christ as he was about to ascend to heaven.

Consider a person languishing in bed, lying at home, worn out with sickness, close to death, his breath in shallow gasps, his soul, as it were, between his teeth. Perhaps he is anxious about something very dear to him, which he loves very much, and it enters his mind. Calling his heirs he says, "I beg you, do this." As far as he can, he struggles to detain his soul so that it does not depart before he can form these words. When he had spoken those last words, he breathes forth his soul. He is borne a corpse to the grave. How do his heirs remember his last words at the very point of death? What if one should stand up and say to them, "I will not do this." What should they say to him? "Should I not do what was the last command of my father as he breathed forth his soul, the very last words which sounded in my ears from my departing father? Whatever other words I had in other ways, surely his last words hold me more strongly since I have neither seen him nor heard his voice again."

Think with Christian hearts, brothers. If, for the heirs, the words of one about to enter the tomb are so sweet, so gracious, of such solemn import, then for the heirs of Christ, what must be accorded to the last words of him who was not about to go back to the tomb, but to ascend to heaven! As for the one who lived and is dead, his soul was snatched away to another place while his body was placed in the earth; whether his words be carried out or not does not concern him. Now he has something else to do, something else to suffer. Either he rejoices in the bosom of Abraham, or in eternal fire he longs for a drop of water (cf. Luke 16:22), and meanwhile in the tomb his body lies insensible; yet the last words of the dying man are safeguarded. What have they to hope for, who do not keep the last words of him who is sitting in heaven, who sees from on high whether they are treated with contempt or not?—the words of him who said, "Saul, Saul why do you persecute me?" Who keeps an account for the judgment of everything he sees his members suffer?

10. "But," they said, "what have we done? We are the ones who suffered persecution, we did not persecute." You are the ones who carried it out, you miserable people—first because you divided the church. The sword of the tongue is sharper than one of iron. Hagar, the handmaid of Sarah, was proud, and she was afflicted by her mistress because of her pride. This was discipline, not punishment. Therefore when she went away from her mistress, what did the angel say? "Return to your mistress" (cf. Gen 16:4–19). Thus, carnal soul, just like the proud handmaid, if perhaps you have suffered some trouble for the sake of discipline, why are you maddened? Return to your mistress, hold fast to the peace of the Lord. See the Gospels are brought forward and we read where the church is spread abroad. This is a matter of dispute and they said to us, "Betrayers!" Betrayers of what? Christ entrusted his church to us, and you do not believe. Shall I believe you when you slander my parents? Do you want me to believe you on this question of betrayers? It is you who must first believe Christ. What is worth believing? Christ is God, you are human; who ought to be believed first? Christ has spread his church

through the whole world: I would say, "Despise!"; the Gospel says, "Beware!" What does the Gospel say? "Christ ought to have suffered and risen from the dead on the third day and that penance and forgiveness of sins should be preached in his name." Where the forgiveness of sins is, there is the church. Why the church? For it was said to it, "To you I give the keys of the kingdom of heaven and whatever you will bind on earth, it will be bound in heaven, and whatever you will loose on earth, will be loosed in heaven" (Matt. 16:19). Where is the remission of sins spread abroad? "Through all nations, beginning at Jerusalem" (Luke 24:47). Believe in Christ! But because you are aware that if you will believe Christ you will no longer have anything to say about the "betrayers," you want me to believe slanders against my parents rather than you believe what Christ predicted.

# IX.

## *Romanos the Melodist*

### THROUGH THE COMING OF
### YOUR HOLY SPIRIT

Prologue.
Through the coming of your Holy Spirit
   raise my soul upright as upon a staff
so that leaning confidently upon this
   I receive aid from you.
Prostrate through the misery of sin
   I look for your pity.
      Since I have fallen through negligence
      Raise me, my Savior, by penitence.


1.  Out of love for men that is proper to you
    You have made me a temple for yourself
    in which you promised to dwell and walk in me.
    But Savior, I have become ungrateful
    having degraded myself and insulted grace.
    Since you are compassionate, you yourself make me new
      again
    causing the all-holy Spirit to dwell in me.
    O Word and only Begotten of the Only One
    God of God who lives through the ages and who bears the
      universe
      Since I have fallen through negligence
      Raise me, my Savior, by penitence.


2.  Your goodness is overwhelming
    for you are by nature the lover of humankind.
    You alone are able to renew the degradation of my soul.

114

Since it is diminished, transform it,
appoint it to be a pure dwelling, a temple
for your Holy Spirit so that I may live out
the remainder of my life in purity.
For all my time has been squandered
in the sins and indulgences of life, for this I supplicate you,
    Since I have fallen through negligence
    Raise me, my Savior, by penitence.

3. Christ, Savior, you are the light,
and the Holy Spirit is light.
As you said before, this is the one
whom you have now sent, according to your promises.
For he indeed has filled the world,
and he indeed has brought light to those groping about in
    darkness.
Through him all the wanderers have retraced their steps,
through him the untutored have been made wise.
This is the one who will strengthen and purify
my soul and mind from all stain that I may cry out to you
    Since I have fallen through negligence
    Raise me, my Savior, by penitence.

4. Your undeceiving promise
copiously and insistently rains down.
For on every side you have showered your grace like living
    water.
Hence temples of idols have been torn down,
hence the garlanded statues have crumbled to dust.
The panegyrics, the incensing, the bacchanalia have ended;
and the very air, polluted by the smoke of burnt offerings,
is relieved at the cessation, and the universe has been taught
the power of your discernment, and I, too, bow before you,
    Since I have fallen through negligence
    Raise me, my Savior, by penitence.

5. This one is both the myrrh that perfumes
    and the fire which consumes the sins.
This is the sword which pierces through the Enemy of the
    world,
A fountain from which gushes salvation,
A tranquil sea whose pleasant waters gives drink to the thirsty.
A river which goes out from the bosom of those who love you
    overflowing the banks of your love.

Having drawn me into it, pierce me through to cry to you
    unceasingly,
  Since I have fallen through negligence
  Raise me, my Savior, by penitence.

6. You who alone are the Most High, have mercy on me,
   You who welcomed prostitutes and publicans.
   For, if I am overcome by many sins, yet I sing to the Paraclete.
   Just as I bow in worship to the Father
   So I bring the same worship to the Spirit
   For he is co-equal and enthroned with and eternal.
   He is the Completion of the Complete and the
       Counsel of him who truly counsels.
   For one is the glory and the authority
   Father, Son and Holy Spirit, consubstantial Trinity,
     Since I have fallen through negligence
     Raise me, my Savior, by penitence.

# X.

## Maximus the Confessor

### INTRODUCTION TO QUESTION 48

Come, Word of God, worthy of all praise, give us the revelation of your words, proportionate to our understanding, and penetrating the density of the veils, show us the beauty, O Christ, of what is to be spiritually apprehended.

Take our right hand—I mean the intellectual capacity in us—and guide us in the way of your commandments (Ps. 119:35); "Lead us to the place of your wondrous tabernacle, to the threshold of the house of God, with a cry of exultation and confession of praise and of the echo resounding of those being festive" (Ps. 42:5); that by the "confession of praise" through deed, and the "exultation" through contemplation, being made worthy to come toward the marvelous place of the unutterable banquet, we may join the solemn feasting by "those being festive" spiritually, as we begin to sing with silent chants the knowledge of the inexpressible.

Pardon me, O Christ, and be merciful, on account of the duty enjoined upon thy worthy servants, as I venture upon that which is beyond my capacity. Enlighten my darkened understanding for the contemplation of what is placed before it, so that by giving sight to the blind, and clear articulation to the slow of speech, you may have all the more glory.

# Bibliography

## ODES OF SOLOMON
Charlesworth, J. H., ed. *The Odes of Solomon.* Society of Biblical Literature, Texts and Translations, Pseudepigrapha Series. Missoula, Mont.: Scholars Press, 1978.

## MARTYRS OF LYON
Musurillo, Herbert. *The Acts of the Christian Martyrs.* Oxford: Clarendon Press, 1973.

## CLEMENT OF ALEXANDRIA
Ferguson, John. *Clement of Alexandria.* New York: Twayne Publishers, 1974.
Mondésert, C. ed. *Clement d'Alexandrie. Protreptique.* Sources chrétiennes. Paris: Editions du Cerf, 1961.

## ATHANASIUS OF ALEXANDRIA
S. *Athanasii, Epistola ad Marcellinum.* In *Patrologia Graeca,* ed. J. P. Migne, vol. 27, cols. 11–45. Paris, 1857; Turnhout, 1979.
Gregg, R.C. *Athanasius: The Life of Antony and the Letter to Marcellinus.* New York: Paulist Press, 1980.

## GREGORY OF NAZIANZUS
*Oratio 38.* In *Patrologia Graeca,* ed. J. P. Migne, vol. 36, cols. 311–34. Paris, 1885.
"On the Theophany or Birthday of Christ." Trans. C. G. Browne and J. E. Swallow. In *A Select Library of the Nicene and Post-Nicene Fathers,* 2d series, 7:345–51. Grand Rapids: Wm. B. Eerdmans, 1978.

AMBROSE OF MILAN

Faller, O., ed. *S. Ambrosii. De virginibus.* Florilegium Patristicum, fasc. XXI. Bonn: P. Hanstein, 1933.

Paredi, A. *Saint Ambrose: His Life and Times.* Trans. M. J. Costelloe. Notre Dame, Ind.: University of Notre Dame Press, 1964.

AUGUSTINE OF HIPPO

Agaesse, P., ed. *Saint Augustin: Commentaire de la première Epître de S. Jean, , 408–39.* Sources chrétiennes 75. Paris: Editions du Cerf, 1984.

Brown, Peter. *Augustine of Hippo: A Biography.* Berkeley and Los Angeles: University of California Press, 1969.

ROMANOS THE MELODIST

Carpenter, M. *Kontakia of Romanos, Byzantine Melodist.* 2 vols. Columbia, Mo.: University of Missouri Press, 1970.

MAXIMUS THE CONFESSOR

*S. Maximi Confessaris Questiones ad Thalassium,* ed. Fr. Comgefis. In *Patrologia Graeca,* ed. J. P. Migne, vol. 90, col. 433. Paris, 1865.

Berthold, G. E. *Maximus Confessor.* Classics of Western Spirituality. New York: Paulist Press, 1985.


For a general survey of Athansius, Gregory, Ambrose, and Augustine, see Charles Kannengiesser, *The Spiritual Message of the Great Fathers.* Vol. 16 of *World Spirituality: An Encyclopedic History of the Religious Quest* (New York: Crossroad, 1985).